Liberation of Being

Allowing Terminal Illness to Teach Us How to Live

By Dr. Dylan Shanahan

"Dylan is showing us the capacity to hold what can only be called a non-dual perception, one that is literally on the razor's edge between life and death itself. He is holding both as two poles of one reality, seen clearly and articulated in exquisite language. That is why everyone should read this book. Because it's real. It's as real as it gets, and it's as profound as it can be."

Brandt Stickley
Professor of Chinese Medicine at
National University of Natural Medicine (NUNM)

by Kimberly Warner

Let's be clear up front: Dylan's story isn't the typical Hollywood redemption arc we've been conditioned to want. Our hero dies in the end. Not now, as I'm writing, perhaps not even yet as his book lands on shelves, but we know without doubt that his body ultimately succumbs to the ravaging wildfire that is ALS. And yet even as the physical diminishes, the spiritual expands. "He shall overcome" is a nuanced, quiet process in this instance—one that I argue is inversely and exponentially proportionate to the rapid decline of matter. A star collapses into itself and produces a supernova.

In September 2019, I had the privilege of meeting Dr. Dylan Shanahan, my first subject in the Unfixed documentary production. Dylan first reached out through a general casting search and contact form on my website. The idea of living "unfixed" is not that popular in our fix-it-obsessed, answer-driven culture. But Dylan resonated immediately and shared that a film dedicated to the topic is much needed in our society. After an exhaustive chase to cure my own rare, neurological disorder—Mal de Débarquement Syndrome—that had gutted my previous identity and left me isolated for years, I was thrilled to have found a comrade who understood the journey.

Dylan was also quick to elaborate on his willingness to participate within his abilities, stating, "I'm in a wheelchair and I speak through a tablet with an eye-tracking camera, Stephen Hawking style." His sense of confidence immediately drew me in as he playfully added, "We must've been friends in other timelines, reuniting in this one to collaborate again. What kind of magic are we going to mix up this time?"

Our first day of filming together was a collision of excitement, fear, grief, and uncertainty—a typical grab bag of emotion for anyone living with chronic illness and disability. I sent Dylan my questions in advance so he could type out responses. Then during filming, his "synthetic voice" would read them aloud. There were many long periods of silence as he painstakingly retrieved each file, pulled it into the proper app, and selected the appropriate commands. He shared the next day that one of the extraordinarily long silences (over thirty minutes passed without a word) was because a film light interfered with his device's ability to track his eyes. Dylan was unable to communicate ANYTHING during that period, so the crew sat patiently under the assumption he was slowly retrieving a file. He elaborates on this experience in his memoir and how, while he was rendered completely helpless with the eyes of an entire film crew on him, he chose to face it down as "another opportunity to practice equanimity."

And therein lies the power, grace, and eternal sunshine of this remarkable human being. It is no wonder that early on in our friendship, I renamed him Vitamin D.

Then, in March 2020, the Coronavirus crisis descended. The pandemic interrupted the Unfixed filming schedule, but I was already too deeply invested in learning from the subjects. So, what do people with chronic illness do when life throws us curve balls? We adapt.

Instead of canceling filming until the pandemic resolved, I began sending prompts to the subjects, including Dylan; trained them (or their health aides) to record their responses with smartphones; and shared their lives in collective, edited episodes each month. As his care team's availability shifted with time, I eventually called Dylan with a recording app and he played his response through the phone. It was a strangely intimate experience, feeling his quiet presence on the other end of the line whilst hearing his thoughts read by a computer-generated voice.

For two and a half years, I learned about the subjects' lives. We investigated what it is like living with the uncertainty of chronic and terminal illness. We explored the challenges and the positives that can come from disability. We talked about food, sex, and the holidays. And we dove into more existential questions as well—what it means to "heal," why our stories matter in this world, and whether we'd give up all we've learned from chronic illness in order to be healed.

And while the process for Dylan was never as easy as opening an app and speaking his thoughts, he participated in nearly every single prompt, crafting responses with utmost skill, self-reflection, honesty, and luminosity. Many of his insights made it into the series, but due to the nature of the short, curated episodes, volumes of his words collected dust on an external drive. I knew some of this would make it into a final feature film, but more of it would never see the light of day, and I grew more and more uncomfortable with this truth.

Dylan texted me in the fall of 2022, after a long period of silence unlike our usual communication cadence, sharing that things were "feeling heavy." The motor neurons in his eyes had started to deteriorate. He had previously made the decision to end his life when communication was no longer an option and this date suddenly felt near. He shared, "What do I do with my time with only six months to a year left?"

And that's when the lightbulb illuminated, spotlighting my hard drive full of Dylan's wisdom.

Due to the rapid deterioration of Dylan's eyes, the revision phase of his manuscript required some creative adaptation. Unable to write additional material, Dylan connected me with his inner circle—important colleagues, friends, and family members—who could illuminate additional parts of his story. I uploaded each new interview onto a private YouTube playlist so Dylan could review, and mostly bask in the profound relationships he nurtured throughout life. He no doubt felt maddening frustration during these screenings any time he heard part of his story told inaccurately and without the ability to make corrections—the level of surrender and trust Dylan practices throughout every moment of every day is more than most must face in an entire life.

Reading Dylan's words, we join him in the ruthless and beautiful mess of it all—drawing meaning from what is not said as much as what is. In many ways, Dylan's memoir is a powerful Zen kōan—a thought tool deliberately designed to inject "great doubt" into the mind. As renowned Sanbo Kyodan teaches, and Philip Kapleau illustrates, "A kōan is unsurpassed for breaking asunder the mind of ignorance and opening the eye of truth."

Like a kōan, Dylan's life invites us to simply observe, marvel at its contrast, and consider its teaching. His memoir asks that we drop the parts that want tidy narratives with pain-free understanding, and instead honor our stories with a contemplative heart where doubt and clarity, failure and success, fear and love exist simultaneously.

Dylan's dream to heal others is now manifest—his life story an ineffable and vital prescription to potentiate and accelerate your own Liberation of Being.

My Happy Place

Lying at the foot of the Giants,

cushioned with a bed of moss below,

covered above by the elders of ancient days

towering up towards the light,

there's a gentle breeze,

a soft rustling of leaves and branches all around:

the peaceful sound of a forest.

Content gazing up at the ceiling of branches swaying in the wind,

the deer off in the distance doesn't even catch my eye.

There are no demands, no external expectations,

no one to impress or let down.

No fear of failure, nor desire to be the best.

It's just the sounds of the forest with me in the center,

grateful to be listening to God's symphony.

Dylan climbing a Doug Fir at his Harstine Island home

CHAPTER ZERO

Infinity

I grew up in the Pacific Northwest, on an extremely rural island in the southernmost tip of Puget Sound—Harstine Island. The nearest grocery store was twenty minutes away, over the bridge on the mainland in the small logging town of Shelton, Washington.

Harstine Island is mostly timber forest and wildlands. I was a pretty wild kid, fortunate to develop a deep bond with nature early in life. At any given moment, I could be found crawling around the forest with my hands in the earth, picking through giant tunnels of huckleberry bushes and feasting off their branches when in season. I loved to climb up the biggest trees I could find, so high that I could feel them sway in the wind.

There was one main perimeter loop drive that every resident lived on, which left miles and miles of untouched forest and deer trails in the center for my brother, sister, and me to explore. Our favorite game was to pack a lunch and see how lost we could get. Since the road is a loop around the forest, we would try to guess which part of the island we would come out on.

As long as we walked straight, we knew we would always find the road home.

PART I:

Doing

CHAPTER ONE

In My Skin

As I begin this writing project in the summer of 2020, it has been two years since my diagnosis of ALS.

Commonly referred to as Lou Gehrig's disease, ALS affects the motor nerves (or the nerves that move our muscles). Without nerve stimulus, muscles go unused—they waste away and atrophy. During that process, the nerve damage causes my muscles to twitch constantly like a short in an electrical line causes a light to flicker.

As more of my nerves have become damaged, more muscle groups have begun twitching. When I am in bed at night and my body has twitching going on all over, I feel it and it can be challenging to sleep. Eventually, I will weaken until I finally lose my ability to move muscle. However, because I've lost about fifty pounds of muscle mass from my already slender frame, the twitching is not as intense as it once was.

ALS does not affect sensory nerves. Unlike the paralysis that comes from a spinal cord injury, I still feel everything. As an experiment, you could try to count how many times in a day you brush off your nose, scratch your head, scratch your shoulder, etc. Then you could take it to the next level and see how many times you cross your legs, shift your weight back, or change your arm position to be more comfortable. What would you do if you couldn't escape an unpleasant sensation on your own? Now you can imagine what it is like to be in my skin.

Not being able to move but feeling everything is a unique experience, to say the least. However, I am well-versed in playing mind games that help me stay calm when uncomfortable or even in danger. I've had a lot of time to practice, since long before this illness came on. Always a silver lining.

My muscles have become so weak that I currently have about 13 percent of my normal breath capacity and wear a ventilation mask to help me breathe. The machine doesn't provide any oxygen; rather, it forces regular air into my lungs so they can expand further. Without assistance, my breaths are too shallow and can cause my lungs to stiffen. Then, even with the ventilation, the stiffness would limit my lung capacity and shorten my life expectancy even further.

Because my muscles are too weak to cough, I struggle with mucus buildup. Whenever I need some relief, I have to lean forward and put my head between my knees to get an assist from gravity to get the mucus to drain out. My pulmonologist recommended surgery to open a hole into my throat so tubes could directly ventilate my lungs and suction out excess mucus. They say it will extend my life expectancy from two years to twelve years. However, the increased need for more specialized care and challenges to quality of life that come with the surgery have prompted me to delay it as long as possible.

The diagnosis has delineated my life into a distinct before and after.

I was a pretty cheerful kid and a good student—besides being attached to the praise of good grades, I have always enjoyed learning. I have always been attuned to my body. I excelled at most sports, including dance, early on. It felt natural to express myself through movement. Basketball was my father's favorite sport, so I gravitated toward it easily. That and we had a full court in our backyard. Later, I became obsessed with the social scene revolving around sports, earning me the positive approval of peers—girls especially—to compensate for the inner black hole that was my self-esteem. I was set on becoming a professional athlete and narrowed in on the NBA.

My father was a lot of things, many positive, like being a gifted writer and the inspiration for my own writing. But he was also an abusive alcoholic. I can't give an origin story for my present mindset, even the shorthand version, without mentioning the abuse of my childhood. The details don't matter as much as the truth: the trauma shaped me into the person I am today, if only by teaching me how to compartmentalize my pain. It might have also played a role in the development of this disease process, as there is a theory that elevated stress hormones can lead to CNS toxicity in people who are susceptible to ALS.

Dylan with siblings, Forrest and Willow, at a baseball game

❧

Vikki Voss
Dylan's mother

You know, they say ALS could be related to head trauma. Also, emotional trauma—and he had that, too, from his father.

When Dylan was born, the midwives didn't come for a while because my last birth took a long time. Until they got there, I was up in bed, singing a spiritual song. Just singing and singing…

When my water broke, it shot out like a fire hydrant. Dylan's head must've hit my pubic bone because his heart rate dropped to half of normal and we went to the hospital. I guess that was his first head trauma.

Patrick Shanahan
Dylan's Uncle

Dylan [as a kid] was very energetic, very positive, and very accommodating. He was excited about whatever you wanted to do. And he was a daredevil, meaning he would do scary, physically challenging things all the time— climbing trees, jumping off bridges, catching frogs. He wasn't afraid of anything. He was very athletic. Very happy. Just a joy to be with.

After I visited in 1986, when he was seven years old, I didn't get back until about 1993. So now he was a teenager—handsome, popular, still very positive, very energetic.

His relationship with his father was difficult; my relationship with his father, my brother, was also very difficult. So we could relate to each other on that level. [Bill] had substance issues. He had anger issues that manifested in many ways. I was able to be a sounding board for Dylan, listened to his frustrations, and told him my own frustration. I think it helped Dylan realize that it wasn't his fault.

Vikki Voss
Dylan's mother

Dylan was so in his body at a young age. He climbed ladders before he could walk, did flips onto a pillow chair, and later off the rope swing. He did all the sports. Once in Little League, he did a cartwheel coming into home plate. He wasn't showing off—well, maybe a little—he was exuding joy.

He was the first boy in our town to be in dance class all through elementary and made it a cool thing for boys to do. He performed in many Harstine Theater Club plays. He was in one where all the young girls were fairies and Dylan was a centaur that would get them to dance. In middle school, he played Puck in A Midsummer's Night Dream. He is such a Puck. He was a perfect physical specimen, one who climbed Mount Rainier and rode his bicycle to Alaska.

When Dylan's father and I went to see Dylan's football game with Lewis and Clark, his coach said he hadn't seen him in over a week. When we found him, he had quit his resident assistant job which provided free housing and was living in a tent in the woods. Afterward, he decided it was best to take a break from college. As we gathered his belongings, I was so impressed with the system he had set up with all his things organized in lockers all over the school.

He was affected by the state of the country after 9/11 and was overextended as a scholarship student with school, two jobs, and football practice. I don't think there were many other football players with double majors in physics and math. Being overextended was a theme with Dylan.

☙

My first academic football experience was as a senior in high school. Even so, I was recruited with a scholarship to play at a small college in Portland, Oregon. After two and half years there, I found I had no clear purpose in life. Already using marijuana to cope with my trauma, the events of 9/11 acted as an existential catalyst, and I decided to drop out of school.

Dylan with sister Willow at Lewis and Clark College football game

From there, I rode with my cousin down to San Diego, where I met a German surfer in a hostel. We decided to hitchhike down the Baja Peninsula. I had only my surfboard and less than a hundred dollars for what I thought might be a week-long trip to surf with a new friend. It turned out to be the start of a brotherhood—a six-month epic journey without clocks, calendars, or any money to speak of. We didn't even have a tent.

There, on the beaches of Baja while on the adventure of my life, I made a career choice. My parents had instilled the philosophy and ideals of environmental conservation that allowed me to feel a connection to nature. When I initially explained this to my career counselor, she suggested environmental engineering. I started studying physics and math as required but had no real career in mind. Until Mexico. There, I thought more deeply about that desire and how, as long as humans were to continue poisoning their bodies, we would also continue poisoning the earth. As within, so without.

I decided that I would be most effective in the healing arts and soon afterward went back to college in Olympia to finish my undergraduate degree. This time, at The Evergreen State College.

I walked on for basketball and began studying herbal medicine and creative writing. At the end of my first year, I learned about the naturopathic doctor profession and a school in Portland, Oregon, where I could take that path. I was also very interested in Chinese medicine and acupuncture and could study them both at the same time in a six-year dual program. The rest of my time in college was mostly focused on the prerequisites necessary to continue toward that doctorate.

ℰↃ

Zac Merten
Roommate and fellow
undergrad student at Evergreen College

One of my earliest, fondest memories with Dylan was when we were living at Green Terra house—that's what he had named it—next to this really deep, jungle-like ravine that you can find around the Olympia area.

He was a great drummer and played a djembe drum. I had a flat deep bass Persian drum, and our other friend Andy was also very musical. Often, we'd have very intentional experiences, like Sunday morning meditation times and stuff like that. Coming off one of those, the three of us beat our drums and walked down the path into this ravine. And Dylan was singing. I'm quite shy about singing, but Dylan would just open up and let it out. And we were a little train of drummer boys going down into these woods. It was very bonding—a distinct, fond memory I have of both of those guys.

Liam Shanahan
Dylan's cousin

I was always impressed by him in pretty much every way. He was almost twenty years older, so by the time I had any memories of him, he was an adult. Firstly, I mean, physically, he's big, tall, and handsome. I actually had a poster with Dylan on it from Evergreen's basketball team in my bedroom. It was a season schedule and had a team picture at the top with Dylan in it. I don't remember the year or his number. I remember he looked good in the picture.

Patrick Shanahan
Dylan's uncle

I can think of a lot of negative Shanahan traits, but I don't think Dylan had any of them. I had never experienced a country kid that was so full of love. Joy is the word. Growing up in the city of Philadelphia, you had to be tough. Whereas Dylan was really the first kid I ever met who had no defenses. Pure joy, pure love. Even though he was younger than me, he had a great influence on me.

Here I was, an eighteen-year-old kid with this new nephew, and now I'm watching him go through all these phases from infancy to toddler to boy to teenager, and throughout each, he was just such a positive, loving influence.

The best part came when my children fell in love with Dylan. They adored him. Liam especially would lean into him—I never saw them act that way with anybody else. He definitely taught them a love for nature and how to be kind and gentle. He taught them how to pursue curiosity and come out of curiosity with new knowledge and appreciation for things. He was just a beautiful influence on my kids.

ꙮ

At the end of my sophomore year and my first season of basketball at Evergreen, I was growing tired of the cutthroat competition required to make the varsity team. That's when I discovered a Japanese martial art, Aikido. In addition to being a martial art, Aikido is also a way of life—a path to spiritual wholeness and the invincibility of harmony. Aikido aims not to create all-powerful warriors, but to facilitate the development of consciousness blended with the essence of reality through breathing, its philosophical attitude, and the practice of techniques in the training hall and life.

The founder explains it like this: "When an enemy tries to fight with me, the universe itself, he has to break the harmony of the universe. Hence at the moment he has the mind to fight with me, he is already defeated (2:177)."

This philosophy was born from a Japanese concept: 'budo.' Bu stands for the end of arms or war, and 'do' stands for the Way (3:222). Put together, these two characters stand for the responsibility of the practiced and proficient samurai to protect the people. Even further, the karma of the enemy and the karma of the individual are the same. Therefore, to stop the attacker from hurting someone else stops him from harming himself. From this stance, Aikido always first attempts to diffuse all forms of violence without ever escalating conflict.

There are three situations when one should use the martial techniques: when one's life is in danger when another person's life is in danger, and when a minority disturbs the majority (4:160). In order to accomplish budo, the individual must serve these higher principles that release one from the bondages of ego instincts.

These ancient principles were the foundation from which Aikido was created, and I integrated this information into my training. That spring, I made the basketball team and carried this martial way, budo, into the regular season. However, the goal of athletics contradicts the cherished goal of Aikido.

 batch

Christian Hoerr
Dylan's NA sponsor
I met Dylan at a Narcotics Anonymous meeting, which is not specific to narcotics. It's sort of a catch-all 12-step program for people who are struggling with addiction of any kind. I think he was really struggling with his dependence on marijuana and how it affected his performance in terms of basketball, his schooling, and social availability...

Our conversations were really far-ranging. There were times when he told me about some of his history, some of his family history—there were some pretty grievous harms, let's put it that way, handed down by his family of origin. His father was a physical and emotional abuser. There's no question about that. He was a deeply flawed man, and that's putting it generously.

I tried to provide some context and a more balanced view to be grounded in, as opposed to thinking "This is how men are." His father's example was one of toxic masculinity, and for Dylan, there was a quest to find masculinity in a way that was more wholesome and more humane.

๏

As one progresses on the path, the heightened perspective is like "walking along a narrow ledge...it is easy to fall to one side or the other, either into complacency or aggression (3:193)." One of Aikido's main goals is winning without fighting. The Aikido practitioners have no need to assert their dominance in any situation. Hence, one of the main rules of Aikido forbids competitions and tournaments. This is to minimize the potential for desiring victory, showing off, or developing a dependence on technical proficiency.

The only permitted competitions within Aikido are with oneself. Making personal refinement the victory gives one an eternal achievement. Otherwise, the victory over another person must be constantly fed to maintain, resembling a leaky bucket that must be continually refilled. If we can leave this tug-of-war, there will be no need to create a loser, for we will both be winners. The applications of this attitude reach into any and every interaction, because if two people can understand and respect each other's position, then no one is left competing for ground to stand on. This requires a mindset of selflessness, with no fear of loss or death.

In sports, one gains victory over one's opponent. In Aikido, one becomes victorious over the self or ego. To dissolve this conflict, I decided to retire from competitive sports and instead took up training that resonated with my nature and who I was striving to become—a spiritual warrior, with Aikido as the path.

I graduated from Evergreen knowing that achieving my career goals would become a non-stop endeavor, from graduate school to clinical practice. Before turning my complete focus in that direction, I wanted to go to Japan, the birthplace of Aikido, to train in the art of the peaceful warrior.

ભ

Adam Dombrowski
Housemate and
fellow graduate student at NUNM

If I were to boil Dylan's impact on me down to one thing, it's his wisdom of Aikido, an overarching philosophy he had cultivated over a lifetime. Dylan talked about yin and yang and the philosophy of medicine, how this comes into play every single day—with light and dark, happy and sad, high energy and low energy, wakefulness and sleep.

In the practice of Aikido, you use your wisdom of the yin and yang relationship to respond. If someone tries to physically assault you, the philosophy of Aikido is to take it in stride, with grace to move with the punches, so to speak. It's able to turn that energy, which initially feels negative and like something you want to push away, into something beautiful and smooth that you're able to bring into the flow.

ભ

To fund my ability to pursue my true purpose in Aikido, I applied to teach English in Japan, thinking I would be there for maybe two years. Instead, I stretched the stay out as long as I could—for five years, just before a large chunk of my pre-requisites were about to expire. At that time, I became a second-degree black belt as a live-in student at the training hall of my teacher, Hiroaki Kobayashi, and his father, Yasuo Kobayashi.

After that, I returned to Portland, Oregon, and began my first year of medical school at the National University of Naturopathic Medicine as planned. But even during medical school, I continued to visit my Aikido teachers in Japan and stay at the training hall for vacations. I started an Aikido club at my medical school and taught the weapons portion of the practice there. I remodeled my garage into a smaller training hall and began teaching a few friends from school, in pursuit of my dream to share this path with the larger community.

On my last trip to Japan, my teacher surprised me with a scroll of his calligraphy. This is the traditional license to signify that I am a lineage holder of my teacher and have received his blessing to teach under his name.

❦

Excerpt from Dylan's application to live and work in Japan
I am a bridge connecting East and West, modern and traditional, art and science, warrior and healer, and physical and metaphysical.

On one side, I am very rational, deductive, analytical, organized, and adept in the sciences. On the other side, I am spontaneous, intuitive, and free-flowing; I create art; I write and perform music, poetry, and dance.
By bridging the gap between these aspects of myself, I will insert my whole self into society with the purpose of connecting us with a better world for future generations.

Aikido dojo in Japan

I Want Nothing More

I want nothing more than the mastery of my art

I want nothing more than to fulfill my heart

I want nothing more than to free my joy

I want nothing more than to open happiness' door

I want nothing more than to let my spirit soar

CHAPTER TWO

Natural Medicine

Liam Shanahan
Dylan's cousin

Dylan was good at finding ways to move you past your comfort zone. It's like he was always living on the edge. He would ask: what decision can you make now that you'll remember forever?

When I was 11 and visiting Washington, there was an opportunity to jump off this big rock into a lake—a 35-foot jump. I'm a city boy [from Philadelphia], so jumping off a rock into a lake is a little intimidating for me. Dylan did it but I was scared. He said it would be cool and told me, "You'll remember it, you'll remember it." Eventually, I ended up doing it, and it was fun.

One important thing he's taught me—less by telling and more by showing—is that there's really no script for your life, and it's not the end of the world to take a turn down a road without knowing where you're going.

Rachel Karlin
Fellow graduate student at NUNM

There was a garden party for incoming students, and that's where I first met Dylan. We were friends from the first time that we talked. There were only six of us dual-degree students, so we were a natural group with an automatic closeness. Dylan was always so free with his whole heart and willing to go deeper than most people, right from the beginning. He has this ability to go beyond the superficial and jump right to what's important.

Adam Dombrowski
Housemate and fellow graduate student at NUNM

To this day, I think "What would Dylan do?" or "How would Dylan think?" or "How would Dylan feel his way through this? How would he, from his unique perspective, shift through this challenging moment I'm in?"

As someone with acute asthma since childhood, I have been grateful for the symptomatic relief that albuterol inhalers can provide. However, I often wondered how long I would need to rely on buying them—when is Western medicine going to address the underlying cause?

Unfortunately, we live in times where the medical system works better as a business model selling a dependency for chemical symptomatic suppression than it does as a healer curing illnesses. Violence is the chosen strategy in both our medicine and international politics: we try to kill off whatever threatens our safety with bombs and antibiotics.

Both the military-industrial complex and the pharmaceutical industry's priority is generally profit—the same obstructive motive the world faces in addressing climate change. After shifting from an interest in environmental protection to a calling in the healing arts, my part in counterbalancing the profit paradigm was and is the desire to serve, not focusing on my own monetary gain.

My plan after college was to create an NPO community clinic with a natural medicine (NM) retail and research segment, plus an affiliated Aikido dojo. Any earnings beyond the economic viability of our NPO were to be redirected to environmental, educational, and humanitarian projects.

This was a stretch for me while conceptualizing it. In the past, I had to make compromises because of my financial circumstances. As a collegiate basketball walk-on, I came into spring training outperforming nearly all the scholarship players, but after a summer focused on making enough money for the next school year, I lost my athletic edge by fall. Moreover, any discontent I felt while teaching English in Japan stemmed from having only a shallow motivation for the job: to continue my employment only to repay my college loans.

In fact, some of the material I've included in this chapter I first wrote as part of a scholarship application to NUNM, which I needed to continue schooling. I wrote: "As the sun sets, we have but a little light left to work... I desire to be a wholehearted sacrifice on the front lines of humanity's advance into brighter days." And I meant it.

Given the imbalances of our bodies and minds, environment, and economic system, few realize the critical point that all life now faces. Fewer still feel there is anything they can do about it. But I had found my calling amidst society's metamorphosis: as a naturopathic doctor, I could become a call to attention, offering a pathway to health, happiness, and a just and balanced world.

I concluded my application with this: "If my life's work were to increase the availability and quality of NM even incrementally, I would be afforded a window to look back on my efforts with peace of mind and know that this scholarship helped make it possible for such evolution to have been the main priority. For the revolution of society and the globe are as inevitable as tomorrow's rising sun."

ᴄ⁄ɔ

Donald Spears
Housemate and fellow graduate student at NUNM

Before the program even started, we had an email chain where people introduced themselves, and Dylan left quite an impression: he was the only person who included his own poetry.

When I did meet him in person, right away I noticed his presence—he exudes such warmth. He's a bright, shining light the moment he enters the room. He's always willing to share a little bit more.

Shannon Curtis
Housemate and fellow graduate student at NUNM

His house was so beautiful. When I moved to Portland, I remember how cozy it was and exactly what I wanted. I don't even know if I've ever expressed to Dylan how much it meant to live in that welcoming. He had a loft upstairs where he'd study. He had a meditation area and a movement center. Eventually, he built out the garage to be an Aikido movement gym...

On a typical day, I'd wake up and go to the kitchen, and he was already up. He'd have his stuff that he'd make in the kitchen. We'd make our morning drinks together. We'd chit-chat, eat breakfast, and then have school all day.

It was definitely an eight-to-five gig. We'd come home and if we didn't cook together, we had dinner together. We always had time in the evenings for each other to sit around the table and commune. Every week, he'd have people come over for potluck and chanting and movement, to share stories, to share poetry. He always made a special effort. It was a really beautiful place to be.

Mikael Brucker
Fellow graduate student NUNM

He was one of those people that everybody knew on campus. He had a very large presence and personality, so you couldn't NOT know him. But we shared a variety of commonalities and attractions, so we became fast friends. My undergrad was physics, and I know that Dylan really admired that type of thinking—analytical and very logical. He always appreciated having philosophical discussions together.

જી

During my time at Lewis and Clark College, I had been unaware of how to manage the stress I felt. I later experienced the joy and freedom of replacing an external dependency with empowering self-soothing strategies like meditation, healthy foods, spiritual awareness, and the enjoyment of nature. I wrote at that time, "Living a lie is dying each day. Surely, all life is dying, but the rate of decay is a choice of way."

My empathy and compassion for the suffering of others, and my perspective on the health-happiness choice, reached a great depth in those experiences. Like the wounded healer Chiron unable to undo the past, I too felt healed in the process of healing others.

I envisioned a parallel transformation, for myself and the world; reducing excessive condensed energy use like oil, coffee, coal, and meat; growing energy closer to the sun with solar, vegetables, wind, and breath; and finally, patient anticipation as the process unfolded.

જી

Paul Kalnins
Professor and Clinician at NUNM

People call themselves holistic doctors, but they aren't really practicing holism—they're practicing reductionism. That has been my observation of what's happening with the naturopathic profession. They say, "Treat the cause," but it's all reductionistic and using biomedical language.

It's sad, but it's where American healthcare is right now. The way we've pushed it to be something economic, we've equated healthcare with factory work, basically. And as a result, you destroy spiritual connections.

So, I think Dylan was looking for alternatives.

Brandt Stickley
Professor of Chinese Medicine & Pathology at NUNM

Dylan had such a deep insight into the heart of classical Chinese medicine. I'd been given the assignment to write a reflection on a passage from a classical text—really the fundamental text of Chinese medicine—which was, if I'm not mistaken, about the heart. Dylan wrote about an experience at a Qi Gong retreat that pierced through his heart, so to speak. He wrote about it so viscerally and clearly. The paper may have been handed in on the later side, but it made an impression because it was so genuine. And as we all know, that [depth] is par for the course for Dylan.

There's something genuinely, deeply spiritual happening in Dylan's life and mind and spirit. And his sharing of his experience in a context that is so real and pressing is so profound that it beggars description. Every message I get from Dylan is exquisitely true, and so profoundly present and insightful. He reaches for and then finds something that can only be characterized as life itself, seen with great clarity.

Donald Spears
Housemate and fellow graduate student at NUNM

It's like he already knew the philosophy. In our first year, we took philosophy courses...I didn't even know what he was even talking about until maybe four or five years into the program. But that's just how natural it was for him. This philosophy already imbued him. And [he was] so passionate about it. It wasn't just about him. He was there for us in the cohort and the profession as a whole. It's always been not about him but about the whole.

Shannon Curtis
Housemate and fellow graduate student at NUNM

Dylan was so wise. Things that I've spent my life searching for, he was born knowing innately. I went to naturopathic school not even knowing what it meant to be a naturopathic doctor. Dylan knew what the medicine was about, knew what it entailed. He knew it in his heart. You could just see that from day one.

Mikael Brucker
Fellow graduate student at NUNM

You don't go into this medicine if you're not looking for a life change or paradigm shift.

❧

Nature provides us with a window into the mystery of Life. Unfortunately for the scientific community, a window is seemingly invisible, leaving little to be confirmed with diagnostic imaging. Relying on data to verify reality will never give you a wholly accurate understanding of it. It was a paradox, then, for NUNM to be an institution training physicians to practice vitalistic and naturopathic medicine while remaining in the environment and context of disease-oriented primary care.

So, I campaigned and won a seat in the student government. My first speech implored the board:

"Can we embrace the paradox of training us to think like naturopaths, while also learning to communicate and utilize standard diagnostic criteria and standards of care when needed?

Can we expand our understanding of cellular pathology and advance our clinical reasoning skills, while meanwhile solidifying and deepening our understanding and clinical application of naturopathic principles and philosophies?

Can we modernize naturopathic terminology? For example, learning to associate terms like 'the healing power of nature' with 'dynamic homeostasis'?"

After I finished my second year, I talked frequently with the student body about how we could improve the balance of biomedical and naturopathic training, as a large population of the student body including myself were left needing to supplement our four-year training—hundreds of thousands of dollars' investment—to fill the gaps in naturopathic learning. We were taught how to use botanical medicines to treat diseases but were unable to use them holistically without studying outside the school.

I ran for the PCRC position and spent two years promoting curriculum changes that would strengthen that integrity, then ran for student representative to the board, to work to balance our training toward naturopathic medicine and primary care preparation. Attempts were made to rectify the situation and a new ND program curriculum was developed—but the problem runs much deeper than curriculum alone. The inherent pressures on the profession and its educational institutions continue to expect them to conform to accepted medical paradigms and practices.

Yet science is still evolving. Even now, there is a search for the variable to counterbalance gravity. Gravity itself is a mathematical unbalanced equation until we solve it. We've called it the 'Vis', CCM Yang qi, prana, breath of Life. How can we redefine our roots to better resonate with the scientific and social reality of our time? A shift toward a natural approach is already the trend: Cleveland Clinic started a functional medicine center, the field of neuro-cardiology emerged to better understand human beings as a network of integrated systems of physiological regulation, the American College of Physicians suggests heat wraps, yoga, and mindfulness mediation before opioids…

Meanwhile, naturopaths are being trained to only see patients for the diseases they bring with them—to start from the other end of the spectrum and focus on eliminating disease as the enemy, the invader, with a defensive or offensive strategy. The further naturopathic education is stretched into physical biomechanical ways of thinking, the harder that task will become. If we only have a hammer, everything becomes a nail.

ℰℐ

Donald Spears
Housemate and fellow graduate student at NUNM

Come our second year, we had a big course called Clinical Physical Diagnosis (CPD) where we learned about all the symptoms, how to diagnose disease, and then give treatments for those diseases. It was presented very conventionally, all based on symptoms. And then you did conventional labs and imaging—and that's how you got your disease diagnosis.

Dylan was not happy with that. Where were the naturopathic ways of diagnosing? He would chase down our CPD teacher to continue the conversation in the hall because she was just over him continuing to badger her about why we weren't learning more naturopathic ways of diagnosing.

Rachel Karlin
Fellow graduate student at NUNM

We shared the same student government position before his diagnosis. I remember a meeting that we had with the executives of the school, and I remember walking out of the meeting fired up about how important the curriculum committee position was for duals. They wanted to get rid of it, and we were both really fighting to keep it...

I remember in all our meetings—but particularly that one—just how passionate Dylan was about the dual program, integration, synthesis, understanding the big picture, and having the skills of a naturopath. That whole cosmology and how we fit in the bigger universe was important to him. He was so articulate about that and would always fight for whatever he believed in.

ℰℐ

Students are drawn to institutions like NUNM because they want to help change the world. I saw the world dying. I saw our society killing it while sick with suffering. I saw a medical system driven by capitalistic intentions rather than reducing that suffering.

I saw a glimmer of a candle of hope, in a small school that offered what I thought was a different paradigm of medicine. A natural approach to the natural suffering of society, a profession that has rebelled against oppressive forces, refusing to play nice in the sandbox if it meant giving up the cornerstone of healing and health.

I saw the coming wave bringing a return to balance. Not a return to some golden age of living in the trees, rejecting science and technology— but a return to a balance of energy and matter, science and art, mine and ours, suffering and learning.

Then again, as Upton Sinclair once wrote, "It is difficult to get a man to understand something when his salary depends on his not understanding it."

❧

Paul Kalnins
Professor and clinician at NUNM

With every organ process, there's a corresponding soul spiritual process. We all have a primary organ that is sort of weakened—we can say that's the basis of our temperament. And that can be based on our genetics or epigenetics. Getting more metaphysical, we can bring past lives or karma into it, and there's a spiritual element that comes in.

In traditional Chinese medicine and in homeopathy, lungs are connected with grief. Real sadness. I sensed that in him. Right before his diagnosis, he had such a passion for getting these ideas out, and that's what attracted him to the program. People with that kind of lung activity tend to be more academically minded. They want to think in the higher pictures. They're not satisfied with the status quo, which is kind of broken.

Adam Dombrowski
Housemate and fellow graduate student at NUNM

Probably a month or two after he had been diagnosed, [Dylan] had been to a student council meeting, and we were at home in the kitchen, standing around the table. He told me, "Those minutes that I'm sitting there are precious to me right now. And every minute feels like a year being spent. I don't want those years to be wasted. I want those years to be invested. Every moment, every second."

There's No Altar

I walk on this Earth with shoes on my feet, wondering where to sit.

Where's the Sacred space to relate myself to a higher cause?

These rocks trip me up, and I fall to the ground.

Rising up to the sky I ask,

"Where are all the Altars?"

Where am I to talk to God? How am I to connect?

Trees block my view of the horizon,

the oceans cover the secrets held in the depths.

There's no Altar.

I blow out the candle to turn on the light, for some better sight to

read.

Surely there's something in these books to tell me where the Altars

be.

Cemented streets, sky-scraping buildings...

Are these the New Age Altars?

From their tops, I'm closer to the Stars,

walking the streets my new shoes stay clean,

though I still feel no closer to an Altar.

I've been into every shopping mall, supercenter, QuickyMart,

drive-thru, downtown, and no one has an Altar for sale.

I'm tired of looking, and there's a rock in this park.

I'll sit right here until it gets dark.

CHAPTER THREE

When the Mic Drops

Patrick Shanahan
Dylan's uncle

One of my best friends died of ALS. I went through that whole process, the whole five-year process. So I knew what was coming for Dylan. Even though I was just seeing him with a strange arm sensation at the time, I knew that it was going to become two arms, and then a foot, and then a leg… It starts with your extremities, and it just keeps going. I knew what he was in for. I was scared, you know? I wanted to hear him say what it was… I wasn't going to be the one to say, "This looks like ALS."

ε∕϶

It began with a frozen shoulder—my right—and then traveled down to my dominant hand. It took about a year to figure out what was going on, so I had many months to warm up to the possibility before the mic actually dropped. Around that time, we also found out my father's melanoma cancer had metastasized to his lungs, and he was starting to unravel. So, I extended my last year of school into two, to help manage his affairs.

I never really let it in, though, the idea of ALS. If it was just a leading theory, I could look at it but keep it at a distance.

Eventually, after my right arm weakness worsened and nothing else was working, I was referred to a neurologist. Ironically, I was hesitant to see him because I worried I might need surgery. But then the MRI results failed to provide any smoking gun, and he suggested I may have ALS. Suddenly, surgery didn't seem like such a hard conversation. It's all relative.

There was some shock at that point, to hear a doctor say he thought I had a terminal illness of total disability and no cure. But ALS itself was far too rare for him to diagnose alone, so he referred me to the neurologist across town who specialized in ALS. I could continue to brush the whole thing off with a dismissive, "He clearly doesn't know what he is talking about!" I still had an out even when the ALS specialist told me that it was her leading suspicion, though I didn't fit the diagnostic criteria because I didn't have multiple limb weakness. She even had an alternate diagnosis possibility we could consider—brachial neuritis, an inflammation of the main nerve that goes out to the arm in the shoulder.

It was a pretty stark contrast of possibilities: either a benign process of random inflammation or a terminal illness. If the former, I'd likely be fine. In a few years, as with most with brachial neuritis, I spontaneously recover and fully regain functioning. But if that latter, I might be entering into an incurable disease process. At least one source I read told me ninety percent of people died from ALS within three years. In this case, the nerves extending to my muscles would progressively die off, taking first my limbs, then the muscles that allow me to eat and speak, and finally the diaphragm, which enables breathing.

I felt like Schrodinger's cat: both alive and dead. Perhaps that's why I felt the need to try to hide my unusable hand and twitching muscles—if the cat is observed, then he is already dead.

I remained hush-hush about my symptoms and what they might mean. When my family asked about my appointments or discomfort, it was difficult to lie to them for such a long time, but the truth felt like too much to lay on them without knowing it for sure. So I found a middle ground: I would simply say that my doctors didn't know what it was— which was not completely untrue, since they hadn't diagnosed it yet.

All that waiting left the door open for me to research what else could be wrong. I got really excited at the possibility of having a special type of lung cancer that secretes hormones, called paraneoplastic syndrome. I felt a lump in my chest and remembered learning about this type of cancer in our pathology class. When I looked it up and some of the symptoms matched with mine, I remember both getting excited about the possibility and making a mental note of the rare state I was in, hoping for lung cancer.

It is all relative.

I made an appointment to see my neurologist and presented my theory to her but was disappointed to hear that she had already checked for that with one of the ten thousand blood tests she ran in my workup. Still, she appeased my curiosity by inspecting the lump in my chest and even sent me for a chest x-ray to fully rule it out. It came back negative.

All the while, I kept on going in school, life, and taking care of my dad.

And little by little, my left hand began to feel weaker.

I told myself that I was imagining it for as long as I could, but it soon became undeniable. I went to my follow-up with the neurologist feeling like a dead man walking. She ran some tests to confirm that diminished nerve conduction was the cause of the symptoms I begrudgingly reported. It was.

The moment of reckoning had officially come, in April of 2018.

I had ALS.

℘

Adam Dombrowski
Housemate and fellow graduate student at NUNM

I had just finished a clinical shift and we were in the charting room, finishing up our medical notes. [Dylan] walked in and sat at the computer next to me. He had just gotten back from the doctor... I remember him pausing before he said: "ALS." It made me kind of take a deep breath in, and just fill up with air. I turned to the side and really... kind of just... let that moment happen.

And I saw a look of extreme presence in his eyes, knowing what this could mean.

Brandt Stickley
Professor at NUNM

As I recall, the very first symptom was a twitch in the shoulder. I know at that time Dylan was being treated by a trio. He would report to me the things that other practitioners were sharing with him, and their interpretation of what was going on.

As is my way, I sometimes perceive things visually in people's bodies, and I don't decide what that means, but I share that with my patient. Then they make sense of it, or we try to understand what it could mean together. We were pursuing this on a physical level. We were pursuing this on an emotional-psycho-spiritual level. We were trying to see what meaning this could have.

With Dylan, I saw that there was something like a crowbar connected to his shoulder and then came down across his body into his spine, into his vertebrae. I think we came to some conclusions about what meaning it could have, but I don't think I could have been as cognizant of its connection to ALS at that time as I am now, given the central nervous system aspect of ALS.

It didn't start out very alarming, but its persistence proved more and more so. It's like the Hemingway quote about catastrophes, I think: "They happen slowly at first and then all of a sudden." That's certainly my sense of it.

Mikael Brucker
Fellow graduate student at NUNM

It just didn't seem possible. He had a boyish quality to him, even though he was eight or ten years older than me. He always had more energy than me. He was always more excitable. He seemed younger and stronger than me. And you couldn't imagine a diminished physical capacity from him. It was shocking, surprising... kind of all of the above.

Donald Spears
Housemate and fellow graduate student at NUNM

He was so elegant and natural with his movement. There was a basketball rim on campus, and we would shoot hoops in between classes. But often I just wanted to watch Dylan... it sounds cheesy, but everything was just poetry in motion.

And even more astonishing was to see him in nature. We'd go on hikes, and he was like a kid going down the pathways, doing jumps and spins from rocks and tree branches. Just so playful. Like he was a part of it. I enjoy a hike—the scenery is beautiful and being in nature is healing, but I like to go home. For Dylan, it was like [nature] was his home...

When they threw out the diagnosis of ALS, it felt like a doctor doing due dili-gence. "There's no way that you have ALS"—I think that was my first response. I kind of brushed it off. "I think they're just being conservative... I think they're covering their bases." It came as such a shock. And how quickly it progressed...

I think we all felt closer to Dylan, realizing we were going to have to start reaching out more. Dylan almost always took the lead—organized our getting together, fostered community... And when that happened, his friend group came together and enmeshed him in love and compassion.

ᘒ

As I became more and more open about the diagnosis, people want-ed to help me with meals, donations, and helping me around the house. The gravity of what I was undertaking seemed to immediately cut out any superficial worries about what others thought about me. I had to open up to receive help.

It was an otherworldly stretch of time for me.

Hard to believe, but in a six-month span around my diagnosis, one of my two dogs died, one of my two cats died, my mom's mom passed, my dad's dad passed, my dad died, and my marriage died. My ex-wife left me four months after my diagnosis, bringing up major issues of betrayal and abandonment. It was the dark night of my soul—and maybe a bit longer than a night. I felt like a ghost of my former self, in a deep cycle of denial and escapism. I started having panic attacks, especially at night when I couldn't distract myself from the feelings that I tried to avoid.

I started to rely on some of my herbal allies to cope and sleep: skullcap, oatstraw, passionflower, and lemon balm were my go-to's. For more extreme nights, I would incorporate kava kava or valerian. All of them help calm the nervous system and take me out of fight or flight mode.

Thankfully, this was also when I experienced the heart of medicine.

I made an appointment with Dr. A, a practitioner of Chinese medicine, on his next available slot. I'll have to remain rather protective of Dr. A's true identity because the medical system has rules against that kind of healing expression, and Dr. A and I were, and continue to be, very close. He was a lighthouse for the times I was lost, needing life guidance. He was a doctor of life.

Chinese medicine and acupuncture have their roots in a philosophy of treatment meant to restore the health of the body, mind, and emotions. Clearing the impediments allows the spirit's natural vibrancy to shine forth, like the wind clearing the clouds from the sun. I was a bit nervous before my acupuncture appointment that day, however, because I also believe that the treatment is an invitation to sit before the mirror of your soul. With the help of the practitioner, you can see the truth of yourself as well as the false image you've been projecting. I knew I would see a lot of fear in the mirror, and I was more comfortable not dealing with it.

I was straightforward during the intake interview with the student intern. If I kept to physical complaints, it would delay me from dealing with the impending ocean of despair. Then Dr. A came into the room, the student intern brought him up to speed, and he asked me if there was anything else to address today. That was the turning point: I had to choose whether to be honest with myself and him or continue to suppress my feelings.

As was my practice, I strove toward total openness, including the vulnerability that comes with it. I expressed how panicked I had felt since my diagnosis, among other similar topics, and then climbed onto the treatment table.

While I lay on my back, Dr. A began palpating my energy meridians, finding the points he wanted to use. He inserted the needles in my arms and legs. He instructed the student to massage along my kidney channel because fear is an expression of the kidney process. Surely, the ancient masters of Chinese medicine didn't know much about the adrenal glands that sit on top of the kidneys. Or how cortisol, the main stress hormone, is synthesized in the adrenal glands, as well as the shorter-acting neurotransmitters that are part of the stress response.

The student began massaging along the kidney channel. Dr. A had to check on another patient and said he would be back shortly. I began relaxing into the moment, letting my breath be my guide.

Before I describe what happened at this specific appointment, I must give you a bit more background information. I had been practicing trauma-tension release exercises (TRE) with Doctor Tamara Staudt. These techniques stem from observing nature. After a gazelle narrowly escapes the jaws of a lion, when it is safe it will vigorously shake out the trauma-tension. In this way, animals immediately clear it from their fascia, the connective tissue sacks that hold muscles. Only one animal, humans, tends to hold on to our trauma tension, even protecting it.

At first, it was like a usual TRE session, but soon it grew well past anything I had experienced, and then some. What began as a tremor in my hips rapidly grew into a volcanic eruption. My legs were bouncing around and my torso was jerking about. There were rhythmic pulses going through my whole body. The student took a step back. She was also trained in TRE with Dr. Staudt, so the intensity of my shaking was not completely outside the realm of the possible. As the one experiencing this though, it was becoming increasingly overwhelming.

There is a technique to bring yourself out of the shaking if needed, but I was unable to use it. Thinking it was out of control, panic crept in. What I could control was my breath, so I used it to anchor me through the storm. The waves continued to move through my body. At the crest of each North Shore-sized wave, my acceptance of the experience was deeply challenged. After ten minutes or so of this, Dr. A came back into the room. He looked at me in a seizure of sorts and said, "Alright, good," as if this was part of his treatment plan. He began to further stimulate some of the points with the needles. He removed some of the needles from points that were finished, adding a few more elsewhere. All the while, my whole body was still convulsing. It was like doing acupuncture while riding a horse at full gallop.

I watched in amazement as he glided around my bouncing body with ease. He told the student to hold my kidney-one points, the ultimate root of our being, which lies in the middle of the bottom of the foot. Then Dr. A said I was doing great and leaned over me, giving me a kiss on my forehead. I had my eyes closed, but I could "see" a golden glow around my forehead when he kissed me. At the same moment, I felt a subtle rush of warmth go through my body.

This was the very heart of medicine. Dr. A and I had talked at length about the abuse by my father, both physically throughout my childhood and mentally and emotionally my whole life. What could be more healing for me than an expression of pure paternal love? Dr. A stepped out again while the convulsive waves were still going through my body, but now I was more at peace with them. I was still very uncertain about my future with ALS, but I knew I would be protected and cared for. Over the next ten minutes, the shaking gradually sputtered out. What needed to be released had clearly been discharged. Dr. A came back to remove the needles, and we finished the treatment with a warm embrace.

Surely standards of care should not be rewritten for all doctors to kiss their patients, but that was some of the most profound healing of my life. Can we hold the vision for a medical system where a type of intimate connection is possible, even the norm? A medical system that not only tolerates the mysterious nature of healing but embraces and actively explores it as much as we do the known world?

Let us be honest: If medicine is the ocean, we understand about as much as Puget Sound. And yet, we are masters of inference—what we learn in Puget Sound we can surmise how it would apply in the ocean. Similarly, what we are able to do with our medical system is remarkable, but we have not begun to grasp the essence of the ocean. Our capacity to understand the mysteries of life will always be limited, but that is not an excuse to not ask those questions.

There is comfort in looking at blood analysis, a CT scan, or a sputum culture because we know how to understand the physical signs. But what can medicine offer to those who suffer without physical signs, or those like me who have unexplained disease processes like ALS, or like my unfixed brother Brian whose immune system is attacking his digestive tract for an unknown reason? What can medicine do when it can't see the problem or see the solution?

I believe the answer is to begin to look past the physical elements of the human experience to see other layers. Something like Rudolf Steiner proposed in his anthroposophical medical system, where the human is seen as a physical layer or mineral aspect, a subtle energy layer or the fluid aspect of chi utilized in Chinese medicine, a mental layer or our astral influences, and finally a core of consciousness or spirit.

Only if we begin to see the whole human being can we hope to reduce suffering.

To allow the higher processes to unfold.

To progress human evolution, spiritual evolution, the purpose of life...

And the heart of medicine.

Loneliness

Alone

I step out into the night.

The isolation of the emptiness I feel inside,

like being the last soul alive.

The need to fill it with companionship,

so strong I'd pretend in a room of mannequins,

until I return to the truth of my illusion.

There is always the inevitable return.

I can only hide from myself for so long.

There's no escaping the homesickness that settles in,

like a fish out of water,

like plants' roots out of the dirt.

There's always a return or the sickness takes you

to the ultimate return.

So I must face this, in this life or the next.

How to fill this emptiness?

I've tried marriage. I've tried career. I've tried drugs.

None could sustain the fullness that I seek.

I'm alone to struggle with this demon of separation.

There's no helpline in the moment of truth.

Where is the seed that will sprout in my darkness?

To give light when I have lost my way,

to sprout into the love I always longed to give myself,

a gentle guiding whisper when I forget my place.

How can I help this take root,

to weather the storms together,

the harsh climate of my persistent fears,

to be full, so overflowing that I can water your seedling,

so connected that I can brave the forty days,

to eventually return,

as big as the final but with time left

to sing at your homecoming party?

Together.

Dylan and his dog Kokoro

CHAPTER FOUR

The Things We Can't Fix

Roger Batchelor
Acupuncture Professor at NUNM

He talked about climate change and global warming, and he's talked about that in his writings, even though he had a lot going on. I think that was [him] thinking like a physician, thinking like a doctor for the patient: "What is the thing that is most affecting us on every level? Physically, emotionally, spiritually, on this planet."

I'm surprised by the progress and the opportunities we've been able to make... and some things that have happened politically in the last few years have been encouraging. But at the time he was writing, it was like nobody was doing much of anything collectively. For me, that was the most striking thing. Here's a guy who's really going through a lot, and he is noticing this bigger problem.

☙

To give you a better idea of my progression with ALS, let's survey my relationship to food.

Visit from neighbor kids at Harstine Island home

In the beginning, when my shoulder froze and right hand weakened, it only affected me when I ate sushi with chopsticks. After eight months, I'd taught myself how to use chopsticks left-handed and was once again free to eat without limitation. Except for steak. Cutting single-handed was not something I ever learned how to do. But when my left hand began weakening, my relationship with food had to change dramatically.

Initially, I entered what I will call the burrito phase. You can put anything in a tortilla and mix it up with a lot of different flavors. Then I could wedge my weak left hand partially around the burrito and use the table as my second hand. That way I could hold it vertically and eat it down to the table.

About this time, my friends at school started a meal train campaign for me. I was literally nourished by the love of my community. People brought me a lot of wraps. In this phase, it was often a breakfast burrito, various wraps for lunch, and then a normal utensil-required meal for dinner.

I like to have regular meals and can be rather stubborn about certain things, so despite the fact that the fork and I didn't work well together, I refused to give them up. While others ate casually, they were unaware that inside me was the equivalent of an Olympic pole vault attempt to get each bite in my mouth. I would often finish dinners not because I was full, but because I was mentally exhausted from focusing so intently to get the fork to my mouth.

After this, I entered the pureed soup phase. For breakfast and lunch, someone would position the mason jar of soup in front of me with a big metal straw, then I could lean forward and drink it down. But I still didn't want to give up real dinners. So, it was round about this time I finally dropped my pride and let people feed me dinner. Amidst an almost endless stream of humbling experiences brought about by ALS, having someone feed me remains one of the most challenging.

Next was the bacon phase, defined by my tongue and swallowing muscles weakening, which led to food getting stuck at the back of my throat. This would set off a coughing spree that looked like I would die from implosion. I knew that it always passed, but the onlookers' faces would fill with traumatic worry. So, I decided to give up solid food—it was no longer worth the risk or the discomfort of people around me. Except for bacon.

At this time, I became very proficient in doing acupuncture with my left hand, and I relearned how to do my physical exams that way. As the lead student intern, I had to be patient with typing my clinical chart notes out. I had to get creative to keep up, utilizing voice-to-text software to get the bulk of my writing completed.

I also made a lot of creative adaptations to be able to use the bathroom while on campus and in the clinic. I had stopped wearing underwear, and my mom sewed a loop in my pants so I could position my left hand in it and use my remaining shoulder strength to push my pants down. Eventually, I had to get my friends, sometimes even random students, to come assist me—I'd had enough of not being able to get my pants down in time.

My muscle weakness snuck up on me. I was adapting and adapting until I couldn't. It was a pretty serious fall that first opened my eyes. I fell backward on my deck and hit my head on the corner of some siding, requiring a trip to urgent care to see if I needed stitches. It was clear I couldn't be left alone anymore, and I had to scramble to get something in place, still months out from getting the big, slow bureaucratic wheels of Medicaid to churn me out some caregivers. While waiting, I sent an email to my friends from school asking for help with a weekly sign-up spreadsheet. I stopped driving at that time as well, so I also asked for transportation to and from school. Within the first few hours, over half the week was covered. It was an astounding show of kindness and support.

During the fall quarter of 2018, I transitioned to a wheelchair and was given a scribe for charting and to assist me with the physical exams I thought were warranted. Once the process of transferring to the toilet and back to my wheelchair became too precarious, I transitioned to wearing catheters. Similarly, getting in and out of the car became too dangerous, so I started taking medical transport to campus and the clinic.

As my muscles progressively weakened, it eventually became hard for people to hear me talk. That was the final nail in the proverbial coffin of my formal education. I could manage all the accommodations I had been given, but I couldn't ask my patients to struggle to hear my whisperings.

Finally, I made one of the hardest decisions on this journey: after six and a half years of studies, and just two quarters from completing my two doctorate programs, I withdrew from medical school.

❧

Adam Dombrowski
Housemate and fellow graduate student at NUNM

It's remarkable that [Dylan] stayed in school as long as he could and persisted with the dream of being a healer. And that was one of the most impressive things, too, is he had his dream. Most people don't have a vision or dream for what they want, what they believe in—not only for themselves but for the world. He had that. He knew the world that he wanted to create... and he knew it started with himself.

❧

It has become clear to me that some of our deepest lessons come through hardships. Pain on all levels sharpens one's attention, as one potential explanation. I would not wish what I have been through on anyone. At the same time, I have learned so much about myself through my experience, it's hard to imagine how I could have gained it otherwise. ALS has brought me face-to-face with the evolution of my soul. Within struggles, we can find a lotus in the mud, a lesson to light the way toward our growth. It is critical to remember to look for that light, to see past the pain to the potential help the experience provides. This becomes an entire worldview—believing life is always trying to help us, even when it hurts.

I've been working toward the same goals and aspirations since long before this journey with ALS began. What changed is, that with the other aspects of my life removed from possibility, my goals became more essential. For better or worse, I'm not going out for pizza with friends anymore. This life I'm in has been stripped down to the core.

Every time I am aware of fear arising, it is an opportunity to reorient myself from the false identity of my small self that clings to survival to experiencing the deeper truth of who I am. I am on a path. In Chinese it is called the dao, the way. It is simple: through countless lives, we continue this spiritual evolution, which drives our physical evolution, always growing closer to the ideal of love—emulating the masters (Jesus, Muhammad, Buddha, and many more) and following their guidance to advance on the path as they have.

A few months after I withdrew from school, one of my faculty collected testimonies from my peers and petitioned the board of directors to award me honorary doctorate degrees. This allowed me to participate in commencement that June, as I had been on track to do, and I even gave a short speech at the ceremony after receiving my degrees. It was a wonderful experience, which strengthened my resolve to replace a fear of death with love for existence, of which I will always be a part.

෨

Dylan's graduation from National University of Natural Medicine

Dylan's Doctorate Speech

First, I'd like to thank Dr. Saunders for petitioning the board on my behalf, and my colleagues who wrote letters of testimony for me to receive such an honor. I accept these degrees at a time of massive uncertainty. How society will make the twenty-year window to reverse climate change is still unresolved. Numerous solutions to social issues, from growing poverty to lagging gender inequality, from gay rights to gun violence, all remained unclear.

For the last couple of years, I've been looking out from the edge of the cliff of the great unknown. Do you know what I've seen? The goodness of the human heart staring back at me. I completed the diagnostic criteria for ALS last spring after enough strength had faded from my one usable hand. A couple of months later, a good friend asked me a question I would have no answer to: what are you going to do when you can't use either hand? All I could say was, "I don't know." After a few more months, it had become my reality. I could no longer lift a fork to my mouth. And how have I managed? I can say by the kindness of others, I am alive. Surely I might be an extreme example, but I consider it a personal lesson of a universal truth.

Life is symbiotic, and love glues it all together. When the web is tested, its strength is revealed. I gratefully witnessed and received the compassionate strength of this NUNM community, faculty, doctors, friends, mentors, colleagues, and staff from all over this school—the ones I've known as family and the ones I recognized from passing in the hall. I thank you. Thank you for the meals, the donations, and the countless cards and messages of support. I am alive, supported by other life. And that is why the emphasis in Chinese Medicine is to nourish life. It's so true for us all.

I have come to appreciate how essential these connections are when we have all the distractions stripped away. When the meals lose their flavor even our possessions become clutter and dead weight. What is left to value? But the relationships we have with ourselves and each other, appreciating our profound interconnectedness—the ultimate currency exchange. We can understand the depth of the blessing to be embarking on this journey of service to patients, service to life. We have the opportunity to strengthen the threads of humanity with each new relationship that walks into our practice and into our lives.

My understanding of holistic medicine is not only thinking about the most accurate biomedical or Chinese medicine diagnosis but also listening for the larger aspect of suffering that is taking place within. The separation of body and mind is an illusion. It's our mission to go forth and apply this truth to the medical paradigm and patient care. I thus anoint the class of 2019 as the world's soul-iologists—practitioners of liberation from suffering.

Liberation. Can you feel it?

[Here, a past recording of Dylan was played, singing: Liiiii…ber…a…tion]

I would frequently be riding to school in the morning, coming down Barbara Boulevard, looking out across the Willamette River at the sun coming up behind Mt. Hood, singing that chorus at the top of my lungs. Although it's an unfinished song project, its purpose is fulfilled as it can now sing through you all, and your new practices may be held at the heart of all your relationships to life, with love, both inside and out.

Healthy people make healthy choices. Removing the weight of suffering from the vitality of life, a happy world then rises naturally.

Thank you.

PART II:

Breathing

The Looking Glass

Every chance encounter, every random idea,

Every dreaming image, every life lesson,

All synchronicity, all creativity, all phenomena,

Every felt sensation,

Every physical symptom,

Every mental pattern,

Every weather pattern,

Is the unconscious seeking to be conscious,

The present continual revelation, "habitual intuition."

The shadows on the walls longing to reveal their origin.

It's the alchemical evolution of metals to be gold.

A drop of the ocean held on the wind,

Momentarily glimpsing its source,

Before its re-emergence.

Until we fully embrace the divinity of our true name,

Can the Giver of Names ever be whole?

Inspired by Paul Levy's book, The Quantum Revelation. Habitual intuition is how
Suzuki Roshi described enlightenment.

CHAPTER FIVE

Hard to Swallow

I have a lot of practice with micro suffocations.

Thanks to the weakened muscle in my throat, I have trouble swallowing, which can send saliva down the wrong pipe. Normal people just cough it up with no problem, but I can't due to weakness of my respiratory muscles. I have to focus on swallowing completely so saliva doesn't linger and go down the wrong pipe. I have hedged my bets, if you will, by having my headrest tilt my head forward, which makes it easier for me to swallow.

Still, it inevitably builds up in my lungs.

This is problematic. Since I am too weak to cough it up, it stays longer and festers, causing my lungs to secrete mucus to decontaminate it until it eventually obstructs my airways. And I have such limited breath capacity already. I consider the day a success if I didn't have to take bronchodilators to clear saliva aspiration from my lungs.

My body has changed. I am bony. Certain muscle groups have wasted away faster than others, and with that comes asymmetrical tension on joints. In my neck, it causes my head to turn to the right. I was forever asking people to turn my head back to the center until the wheelchair technician found me a sweet new headrest with four fingers that could be bent to hold my head straight. A major success.

The muscle asymmetry in my shoulders doesn't have a remedy that anyone has discovered yet, however. It causes my shoulder blades, and the scapula, to get pulled off my back. This is called scapular winging because they poke out into the air like wings. Mine aren't in the air, though; they are pressed into the backrest of the chair all day. Because this creates pressure sores, I have people reposition my back throughout the day to alter the contact points on my scapula. They have not become open wounds, and it is important I keep it that way. Once one opens, it is very hard to heal and therefore becomes an infection risk.

Another big success came last week.

I used to use chin controls to operate my wheelchair, but about five months ago, after putting a hole in the wall of our apartment with my wheelchair, I had to accept that I was no longer strong enough to operate the controls. Since then, I've had to rely on others to adjust and move my chair with the attendant controls. This is hard for my mom to do. She is, what you might say, spatially challenged, and it's a tight turn to get my chair up the ramp and into our car. The number of times she would run into things and something would get bent—either on my chair or my tablet support bars, both of which needed to be in alignment for my comfort and ability to communicate—was putting a strain on our relationship. The wheelchair technicians and the tablet specialist made many trips to fix things over this period of time. While mom got a lot better at driving, I tended to only be willing to risk going out if it was important. I spent a lot of time in my apartment.

Now, thanks to Steve Gleason—the pro football player who champions the ALS community—and his investment in bringing this technology to the market, I can control my wheelchair with my eyes through my tablet.

Thank you, Steve!

℘

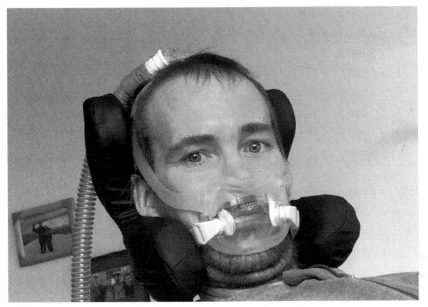

Dylan pre-tracheostomy

Vikki Voss
Dylan's mother

Dylan asked me to move to Portland to help him out in the fall of 2018. I lived with him for over two years until he needed to move into an Adult Family Home. During that time, since the ALS progression was so fast, we developed a motto: every day is a new normal.

We had to be creative with the consistency of his food so he wouldn't choke. And then he would choke, and it would sort of take all the fun out of eating.

When he got the feeding tube, they wanted to start him out on a formula where all the ingredients were chemical names—none were food items. We had to work the system to get him organic formula. I had to say he couldn't tolerate chemical formula, that it caused stomach pains and gas, but I never gave it to him.

Once we got the good organic stuff, I would still make my own formula almost every other day, blending up spinach, eggs, avocados, nuts, blueberries... Some-

times it was a precarious situation, feeding him on the go, in the van, or even once at a Michael Franti concert.

He tried many alternative therapies. Three months of antibiotic therapy, three hours a day through a pic line, to rule out Lymes disease which displays like ALS. At least two appointments a week for acupuncture and naturopathy, with transfers from wheelchair to exam tables. He couldn't help with his muscles, but his legs were like levers, so I got good at pivot transfers.

When we got a van with a wheelchair ramp, we felt we had so much freedom. The medical transport was so unreliable. My daughter, Willow, and I took Dylan on a road trip to see the redwoods of Northern California. We found many wonderful wheelchair ADA trails to see the Giants, though the two of us did have a time getting Dylan from the wheelchair to those tall hotel beds.

I needed help, so we hired and trained caregivers. It was stressful agreeing on when the new caregiver was ready to be left to work solo. I desperately wanted a break, and Dylan wanted to be safe.

When he got his trach, I could no longer do pivot transfers, as his trach was in the way. Not all of the caregivers were strong enough to transfer him, so he had to start using the Hoyer lift. It was a two-person operation to make sure his airway tube would not get pulled. There were times when the caregiver would not show, and Dylan was stranded in his chair until we could find someone to help.

For the night shift, I would drop my mattress next to his bed, and in the night, he would say through his computer, "Suction please," and I would jump up and cram the tube down his trac and vacuum him out. Every other day I needed to change the inner cannula of his trac, which involved unhooking his air supply, removing the old one, inserting the new cannula, and then reconnecting his airway. Just call me Nurse Vikki.

౷

Some of my other daily challenges are around the elimination of my bodily waste. Not the most glamorous of topics, but while we are keeping it real, let me tell you about it.

I am not sure how much longer I can continue the way I am going. I have a spastic bladder, where the muscle around it, the detrusor, contracts more than it should, so I urinate frequently and with urgency. To compound matters, the voluntary muscle—the sphincter that holds the urine in—like all my muscles, is weakening. So I am, more or less, double incontinent.

As with most things, I've developed ways of adapting. I try to urinate at the first, slightest feeling that I need to go. This has not been as effective as of late, so success for me is anytime I have a dry urination. I'm wearing a condom catheter when I have company or when I go out, but I'm starting to have enough incontinence to need some other solution.

Similarly, I have all sorts of challenges with bowel movements. To fully excavate the bowels, you need to be able to bear down. Those core muscles are so weak that I have difficulty initiating the bowel movement. I'd commonly feel like I need to go, then just sit there for long periods with nothing coming. It is a lot of work to get me on the toilet and back in my chair with nothing to show for it. I started to use glycerin suppositories to stimulate bowel movements. I never imagined that I would be using suppositories, but there are too many unimagined things like that to count now.

My bowels have gotten even more complicated lately. Last month, I had the stomach flu, commonly diagnosed as gastroenteritis, and ever since then, I have had loose stools. I went from not being able to have a bowel movement to not being able to hold it back. I have implemented a new strategy to simply stimulate a bowel movement as soon as I get up.

My daily success is taking care of business, while only taking one shower a day, not two. Truth be told, I can't actually get into my shower anymore. I have to suffice with bed baths, which consist of someone putting towels under me and giving me a scrub down, rinse with wipes, and then dry with towels.

We are going to look at buying a place with a walk-in shower—or, for me, a roll-in shower. Until then, we work with what we have.

I remember when I was too proud to let others feed me when I would stop eating because I was too tired of struggling with my fork, not because I was actually full. Look how far I've come, in a little over a year.

A bonus: since I have had plenty of suffocation training, I feel no need to further accelerate my progress. Thanks to ALS, I am already on the fast track at the school of spiritual growth. Additional courses in serenity with airway obstruction bring my credit into overload.

I can space things out a bit.

❧

Brandt Stickley
Professor at NUNM

Listen for the traumatic secret. This is true across cultures, religious traditions, spiritual experiences, mental health crises, spiritual emergencies, and the commonalities that they share—there are events in one's life that crack through the ego, that crack through the self. And the imperative is to take those issues seriously, just as Dylan has shown us. To not try to turn away from the disease, and to not surrender to it unequivocally either.

All life is terminal, as we know. But the immediacy of his turning and facing the reality of it is akin to saying the traumatic experience that creates a crack in the self is not the same thing as the spiritual experience that rushes in through it. And it's equally a mistake to suggest that this event, injurious as it was—this disease, as painful as it is—is not the reason for spiritual growth. It's that this opening… reaches out and connects to something subtle, something unseen by its nature, and invites it into the experience held within the grip of the physical.

Mount Rainier

Pressure is changing, the ante has been collected.

My breath has connected with something greater than me.

Sitting here amongst the Giants. An eagle flight from freedom.

Here is a place where even birds rarely come.

We are making the pilgrimage one step at a time.

Not distracted by the external world.

Listening to the essence that radiates from the exposed glaciers.

I take up too much space in this life.

For we have much to accomplish before the seasons change.

On this journey,

the energy-depleting choices in my life seem like a joke.

There is no real essence to assist my progress.

I am on the edge of the world.

Please open spirit. I am calling.

Wherever I am.

No need for strife, the only end is death.

No rushing the next beginning.

Life, full of love, for all.

Written during my summit of Mount Rainier

CHAPTER SIX

For the Love

I'm going on a trip to Arizona for a wedding.

I'm pretty nervous about flying. Besides my actual health or the pressure and oxygen concentration change at high elevation potentially causing me to have a respiratory emergency, there are so many other things that could be problematic.

I have been in respiratory failure—a diagnostic classification for breath capacity dropping below a certain point—for a while now. I'm at 14 percent of what I'm supposed to have. My pulmonologist has been recommending I get a tracheotomy for a while now. They are pretty surprised that I'm not short of breath, being so low. I think as long as I feel ok, not short of breath, I'll keep delaying the surgery.

It is such a hard choice to get a tracheotomy. If I don't get it, my life expectancy is 1-3 years. With the surgery, it goes up to 10-15 years. Based on that, you might say: Easy, live longer? Get the surgery. But it is not that simple. Ninety percent of people choose not to get the surgery because of the stark challenges it creates for your quality of life. I'd be on ventilation constantly, no longer able to breathe for myself, and the tube in my throat would need a lot of maintenance and my lung secretions would need to be

suctioned out manually. That makes my level of care needs rise substantially. So, it should be clear that I'm delaying for good reason. I'll really need
a strong inspiration to be alive to counter the quality-of-life issues that
accompany surgery.

Back to my decision about whether to fly to Arizona: another concern
was that I wouldn't be able to talk during the flight without my communication device. In the car once, before I had a travel tablet, my arm jammed
when the door closed, so I couldn't move it and I couldn't tell anyone. On
the plane, we won't have a way to set up my device at all. If I get uncomfortable, I would struggle through the guessing game of seeing if they can
figure out what I need.

There was also the high probability of my power wheelchair getting
damaged in storage or during transport on and off the plane. That is a
big deal for me, as I sit in that chair all the time for comfort. If the chair
doesn't move, I don't move. Then, the whole hotel stay without my hospital bed, and whether I'd be able to get my chair close enough to the toilet,
etc.

You might be thinking (as I do from time to time), is it even worth it
to go? My neurologist definitely doesn't think so. But these are really good
friends. The bride was a roommate for a couple of years in the ND program, and the groom was also a dual ND and Chinese medicine student
with me for six years. He is like a brother. Because I'm a poet, they asked
me to share a piece to open their ceremony. What an honor!

So, as could be a slogan of my life now, no easy choices.

I made the trip. And yes, the plane ride sucked as much as I thought
it would. But I survived. Although that, too, was a question at one point.
In the hotel, my brother-in-law and mother slept on beds to either side of
me. But even with two people so close, I was totally alone when I woke up
hardly able to breathe. My head had rolled off the pillow because it was
slanted, which meant I couldn't hit the alarm button to call for help. My
nose was clogged, and my mouth was trapped shut to prevent it from being super dry from the ventilation mask while I slept. I had to wait a long
time until someone finally got up and saw I needed help.

Donald and Shannon's wedding in Sedona, Arizona

This trip, as with my whole journey, was an opportunity to practice surrender and make deliberate choices based on what is most important to me, like being a part of this declaration of union before family and friends.

చు

Donald Spears
Housemate and fellow graduate student at NUNM

We got married on November 2, 2019. [Dylan] had already lost quite a bit of motor function and was relying on his friends and family for support. Well, we got married in Sedona, Arizona, and we invited him. We did not expect him to come, of course, but we wanted to give him an invitation, and he accepted. He, his mom, and his brother-in-law Justin came out, and it was such a magical moment to have him there, knowing what he went through.

That flight did not go well, from what I heard. We can't even imagine not being able to move, being on a plane, having our necks turned around. I think he may have even had a panic attack. It was quite an event for him, coming out there. And it was such a treasure to have him there. He actually wrote a poem, and that's how we started our wedding.

Shannon Curtis
Housemate and fellow graduate student at NUNM

It blew my mind—it blew my mind when he came. I was so grateful. Out of all the things about my wedding, that was the number one thing I was grateful for. And his speech was absolutely beautiful.

At the reception, it was so much fun. Dylan was full of jokes. And it was just nice because we had a lot of our friends from NUNM there and we all got to reconnect. Dylan had his dance moves, you know, in his own way. You could just see he was so happy for us.

I know that plane ride was awful. I know it was frightening. I can't imagine how terrifying it must have been. But despite that, he came to our wedding. Oh, my gosh, it was just such a miracle.

Dylan reading his poem at wedding ceremony

Wedding Poem

Dedicated to the marriage of Shannon Curtis and Donald Spears

November 2019

7.7 billion people on the planet and somehow, we connect.

What cosmic forces are at play, we may never know,

but to what purpose, here we can be clear.

At the forefront of 3.7 billion years

of the accumulating evolutionary process,

bringing us to the threshold of our genetic heritage,

we reach out from the fundamental longing:

to love and be loved.

We choose to embrace this entanglement

against the better judgment of reason,

knowing the safety of our individuality and independence,

we instead let go to the melding of hearts and minds,

like the magnetic attraction of the double helix,

drawing two into one.

Spiraling ascension while pulled ever closer,

surfaces the fears of losing ourselves,

offering the choice to descend into separate camps

hellbent on winning,

claiming the self-righteous territory of victory,

or with great vigilance holding on to the threads of truth.

Trusting that he who does not fight can never lose,

and as long as you have something to defend,

you give something to attack.

It is all given anyway, for love has no boundaries.

Is there anything else more valuable?

If you could choose, wouldn't you choose love?

Today is the first choice of a lifetime to follow.

Trinity of Tones

There is only space,

I am the space.

I am aware, but I'm not there.

Everywhere is the sound.

A repeating series of three rising tones,

of escalating intensity.

I am the sound,

like a string is part of the cosmic orchestra.

The sound is uncontainable.

Do you fear?

Don't worry, you are not there.

Being not there, are you lonely?

Don't worry, there is the sound,

and the trinity of tones.

Let it in,

as you are able.

CHAPTER SEVEN

Inhale Meditation

Vikki Voss

Dylan's mom

When he was going to Lewis and Clark, he went on a couple of retreats with the Hichual People. I think one was around Mount Rainier. One was all the way down at Big Sur. He did several ten-day Vipassana meditation retreats.

He also did a ten-day silent meditation retreat, where you didn't speak. He told me the pain of sitting there for the whole day, but that you work through it. I remember when he came home and he walked in the door, I went, "Oh my god, you're glowing." He said, "Oh, Mom, you should do it."

తు

I have become much more aware of my reptilian brain and its fears of survival. At the same time, I am thinking about my spiritual liberation frequently, and practicing the mind games I believe are removing the obstacles holding me back.

Aikido calls breathing one of the most essential powers. Using the breath to oscillate with the tides of the universal ki, we are fulfilled and can "touch the realm of suchness (8:20)". There is no simpler anecdote for peace and happiness than conscious breathing. While in the dojo, all techniques are carried out with the awareness of breath. Throughout the day, with effort and practice, the continuity of conscious breathing can be a grounding anchor for one's attention in the presence of enlightenment.

I've been thinking about why we don't meditate or do other internal healing practices, and whether it has to do with some sort of resistance. This is assuming we already want to develop our practice and have enough training to know how.

It's easy for me to blame laziness, but that's just my self-critic talking. On a deeper and more holistic level, it seems to be about what motivates us to do things, what system of rewards we depend on or habitually act on, and where we are sourcing our self-worth.

If we seek validation from the external world, the rewards of external achievements and production will drive our motivation to do something. Our resistance to doing internal exercises is the fear that we'll have nothing to show for our effort. The internal arts take much time to progress, and even then, there won't be anything produced to validate my worthiness. How much easier and quicker it is to repair the fence, paint the bathroom, balance the budget, or do any of the various things on our to-do checklists! To get the reward from the external world. To validate our existence. What is there to show for an hour of meditation?

Ultimately, I think we are always doing things because we think we will feel better by doing them. So, it is a matter of reorienting ourselves to the internal rewards and turning inward to the incremental improvements that the internal arts offer us. It seems easy on paper, but undoing ingrained dependence on the external world for our self-esteem rewards is no small feat.

℘

Tammy Staudt
Qigong Professor at NUNM

Some students love Qigong and are thrilled it's part of the [NUNM] program, and others, it's not their thing. They've got a different practice that they're following, whether it's yoga or something else for self-cultivation and movement. Dylan was a beautiful fit for Qigong and really dove into the experience fully.

Qigong, at its core, is the human standing between heaven and earth, supported by the heaven on earth—meaning creator energy above and creator energy below, and how that presence is through a human in this human experience. Qigong accesses that through breath, movement, presence focus, and attention.

There's a saying in Qigong and also in Tai Chi: "Where your attention goes, that qi flows." In the Western world, we tend to be so much in our heads, thinking about things or worrying... And similarly, the energy then is all going out—coming out of our heads and going out around us. It's not settled in our body. As you can bring your presence and your awareness back into your body, you start to truly embody your presence in your human vehicle.

It's moving the physical body as a tool to access the energy—to move the energy of your body. That's not limited by how well Dylan can move the body or not. It's the capacity to tune in to that vibrational frequency where the qi is moving.

℘

Recently, I have been focusing on replacing my negative self-talk with neutral statements free of judgment. I have always been on a quest to know myself and to become a fully self-realized human being. Although that is fundamentally a spiritual endeavor—since what I am is an eternal being, and what is eternal is truth—the truth is also that the macrocosm resides within the microcosm. The spiritual truth of who and what I am is holographically revealed to me through my body. The hard part is for me to keep listening carefully to my thoughts. It is very easy to let my habitual, critical self-talk slip by the guard of my awareness.

For example, I was thinking about some friends that I would see, imagining my response to them asking "What have you been up to?" I heard myself say, "I have been a real bum recently, not doing anything besides watching videos."

Luckily, I caught myself and replaced it with: "I have not had a lot of energy and motivation recently and decided to enjoy some videos while I rested."

While I am focused on my growth, I am living my truth. What could or might happen doesn't matter at the moment, during which I am fulfilling my purpose of becoming.

I don't believe I can choose to label one moment a curse and another a blessing when it is convenient for me. All manifestation is of the source or none of it is, by definition. Sure, that is much easier said than practiced, and that is why I find it helpful to remind myself in the moment that I will decide how to frame my challenging experiences.

For better or worse, we get to decide.

I have always aspired to live in the image of the spiritual masters, however imperfectly I am able. I am not Christian, but I draw inspiration from the stories of Jesus as the full embodiment of compassion—love for humanity and love for whatever word you use for the source of it all. Call it the creator, the Dao, great spirit, God, Allah. I don't think it matters, but reverence of the sacred and love for this gift of life makes all the difference to me.

Choosing reverence has brought light into even a situation as challenging as mine. The sun is always shining above the clouds.

Heiner Fruehaulf would frequently say in our Qi Gong classes at NUNM, "I am in the universe and the universe is in me."

I believe the universe is interchangeable with spirit. My body is therefore a window into my soul. You don't get stronger by staying in zero gravity; it takes some resistance. My body is my training ground, and with the right frame of mind, I don't need to be able to move it in order to engage in training. How great is it to have something tangible to work with to reach for the stars?

It is ironic that I will inevitably feel better after meditating, whereas, with external achievements—especially when it is others' praise that I seek—it might take a while for someone else to notice. That validation might not come at all if what I did doesn't meet their standards or expectations, a common problem for us type-A personalities.

Isn't it a little twisted that the internal arts tend to improve our feelings right away, yet we so often choose the external, indirect route? We overload our to-do lists so much that we end up stressed and let down that we didn't meet our superhero goals, even though the 80 percent that we did achieve would have been a successful day for the mere mortals of the world.

Even if we do feel better with external rewards, it is fleeting, and then we need to keep achieving and producing to maintain the level that provides positive feedback. I get tired just thinking about that pattern; it's like a dog chasing its own tail.

Without tuning in to how we feel, it takes more efforted thought to know we are actually achieving anything besides our mind's confirmation that we are on our spiritual path. And it is true, but the thought is not as satisfying for our emotional reward system, which is the primal driver of our willpower. It's hard to just think your way to self-validated meditation practice—you have to also feel it.

The will to choose to do something has maximal power when we can engage our emotional desires all the way up to our mental faculties that think—and therefore know—that meditation is important to the evolution of our soul.

Meditation has helped me to reduce my stress, improve concentration and memory, and become more aware of my emotions and body. But it is the increased self-awareness that I want to highlight.

What can fill the emptiness that we sought to cover up with the rewards of the external world, other than the heightened consciousness that develops through the practice of the internal arts?

What if the deepened connection to the true state of our beingness, through meditation, could plug the holes in our leaky bucket and replace the desire to perform in order to feel whole and worthy?

Could we finally take a sigh of relief and feel what Thich Nhat Hanh commonly reminds his students: you have arrived? Who among us doesn't desire to come home after a long, strenuous journey; take a deep breath and kick our feet up on the seat of our soul; then say to ourselves, "I have arrived"? After all, we will never get it all done anyway.

That is how I think we can best fully engage our willpower to initiate and maintain the practice of the internal arts, how we can get off the hamster wheel and take action—not to fill a deficiency, but to choose to do something to increase abundance.

∾

Zac Merten
Roommate and fellow undergrad student at Evergreen

During a visit after Dylan had lost the use of his hand, we were out having a blissful time, mostly because he was just so amazing. He had accepted the situation as far as he could at that point, and I think he was really soaking things up. That was obvious—soaking my kids up, soaking up where we live. He was here in a beautiful time of year.

That was early Trump stage, and I was feeling really dark. I kind of wished it would just collapse, you know? Everybody was talking about how "it's going to collapse" and "it's going to be civil war." And I was just tired of it.

I was on this path, feeling hopeless... Like, what world did I just bring my kids into, you know? But Dylan said just a couple of words, it was almost a Zen master thing... Something like, "Yeah, but the suffering that would mean to millions of people? It's not worth it. You've got to change your mind."

I can't say that I haven't descended into some of that darkness since then, but it's not quite the same. He kind of smacked me with a shadow stick.

☙

As in the dojo, all confrontations in everyday life have the potential to refine the self. Throughout the practice session of Aikido, all techniques are carried out as if there were a lethal weapon in the partner's hand. Sometimes there is, and sometimes there is not, but the significance of this type of amplification develops veneration for the lasting effects the resolution of the situation can have on life. These effects can be either beneficial or destructive, and an Aikido practitioner will develop the habit of responding, as the founder says, to "opponents with the power of love, binding them with your affection (1:26)."

Aikido aims to make better people, a better world, and to protect all life. If it only makes someone stronger, gives them better technique, or improves their fitness, it loses its center as a path to social and spiritual peace. Like the lotus flower that grows from muddy waters, the end of WWII gave birth to the rise of Aikido. It is a spiritual path, a way of life, that attempts to purify the raw material of the individual and society—and its creation came at the perfect time when the world was in the depths of an immoral ego bloodbath.

Aikido teaches that one should always approach conflict with the sincerity of a life-or-death situation and the calm of a summer breeze. The paradox of martial art for peace illuminates the interdependence of all dichotomies. Aikido can potentially replace the ego separations in sports, capitalism, and war by necessitating the individual into universal harmony. In the world today, we can see the inevitable revolution that is bound to rebalance power. The corporate elite will most likely attempt to repress this movement with violent force. How are we going to meet this force?

Action, both in the dojo and out, should be toward cultivating positive ki. Starting in the morning, as soon as someone wakes up, Tohei sensei suggests meeting the day with early morning disciplines to bring the dreams that one chooses to create into reality. Likewise, the transition from wakefulness to sleep, from consciousness into the subconscious, can be used to carry positive seeds or pull negative ones from the storehouse of the mind. Then, the remainder of the day we must carry "eyes benevolent enough to do away with the opponent's spirit to fight (4:150)."

Aikido class, Olympia, Washington

e/o

Vikki Voss
Dylan's mother

Dylan and I did have some rough times. We had our routines and protocols, like he wanted me to check in with him before each procedure to see if he was ready, and then confirm and verify my understanding of what he wanted. I would think it was "yes" when it was "no," or forget to verify. Sometimes, I would get into unconscious overdrive, and he would say, "Hey, remember me over here?"

Once, we spent hours trying to get his pillows right. We had no computer, so we used letter cards. I was so tired. We're 45 minutes into it and he says, "Letter card." The first letter is R, which means, "Restart the whole process again." I screamed, "What the fuck, Dylan? What's going to be different this time than the last four times?!"

The next day, when he got his computer back, he said, "You don't need to flip out. I've got to get the pillows right because I'm choking on my saliva." Now I could see his perspective: he is trying to survive, and so he's always planning ahead.

We had counseling over Zoom to work on our issues. He thought I was unsafe and that was kind of hard to hear—that he doesn't think I'm doing a good job. But I learned a lot: that his brain is more sequential than mine, that we both had a need to be heard, that Dylan was looking out for his safety, and I was plain tired. I learned that I did some things that were so wrong in Dylan's eyes, but through my eyes they made sense.

Once, I filmed him for an instructional video without explaining it to him first. It was a bed-to-wheelchair transfer for the caregivers, but he was naked, too.

Another time he gave me the signal for the letter card to explain what he want-ed, but I kept guessing because I hated the letter card. He expressed his extreme frustration by grunting. What did I do? I grunted back at him, mocking his scream of emotion.

He had said that I traumatized him, and I did. The trauma of being disrespected by my anger and frustration. The trauma of being dependent, relying on those with unreliable skills, the trauma of not being heard, and being disrespected by going against your decisions. I have to believe that I abused him because he is certain that I did. I did. He experienced that. But it's also, you know, the fucking ALS.

We had a falling out. I'd been with him for over two years. We had this plan. We were looking to buy a house, and it had to have a room for a live-in caregiver. And one day, after we looked at several houses, Dylan said, "Quit looking for a house. I found a facility to move into. You need to go back home."

He requested a break from our communication. I don't think we spoke for four months or so. Could you imagine that? Then one day he said, "Thank you for giving me that space. How are you doing?"

I'm so happy to be his mother again and not his caregiver.

⚭

There are times when a fight seems to be unavoidable, and in this situation, it can be beneficial to reflect on one's own negativities and bow to the opponent in humble imperfection. Impermanence is the saving grace of our imperfection. If we continue to walk the path, we will one day reach the goal. Furthermore, self and non-self are one, not two. Separation of space, discriminating here from there, are pieces of a reality that has transcended in the moment of now. In the moment's embrace, the goal is realized. What better way to be in the moment than with a full breath of life?

Deep breathing from the hara is a central tool to cultivate Zen or mindfulness. It is like the gardener in the fields of emptiness. What we put our attention on waters the seeds of our choosing (8:129). So what if, with

Aikido, we could guide the corporate spirit into a peaceful world without competition, winners and losers, third-world and developed nations, or heaven and hell? We all have the capacity to breathe this change into the world, with our own determination and faith.

The Mind

Grass Grows Green

Sky Blue

I dreamed of a thought that came true.

Unfeathered flight

I thought of a dream not born in Light

Weed, Water, 'n Wait

The seed will sprout with wings of Fate

Inspired by Thich Nhat Hanh's writings

Dylan visiting his mom Vikki in Indonesia

CHAPTER EIGHT

Exhale Equanimity

My first exposure to the concept of equanimity—to remain balanced between the cravings for pleasure and repulsion of unpleasant sensations—came from videos of Vipassana meditation retreats. The meditation focuses on sensations of the body, and expanding the practice to one's life deals more with the mind. In that balance between the poles of craving and repulsion, I have felt a deep peace.

Of course, the dichotomy of body and mind is an illusion, but it helps to illustrate the significance of using equanimity in daily life. We are constantly labeling situations as good or bad as we do with sensations—either pleasant or unpleasant. In relation to chronic disease and terminal illness, we can't always see the lessons and growth that could come through the experience. For the growth of the soul, the experience with this disease could be exactly what is needed.

Don't get me wrong; I am not being fatalistic. When they told me that I was diagnosed with an incurable terminal illness, I tried everything in hopes of finding a cure. The difference is that my relationship to the disease process didn't change. I made my peace with it while I was searching for a cure, and I have made my peace with it while I live with it and pray for a miracle.

☙

Vikki Voss
Dylan's mother

When I found out that Dylan had ALS, the first thing that came to my mind was, "Okay, I think I need to become a shaman and heal him."

I took an online class from a shaman, Sandra Ingram, that taught about traveling to the unseen world or entering a tree and moving down the roots to speak to helping spirits or power animals.

But I'm not very good at visualizing. I couldn't even imagine walking down a path, let alone traveling down roots. After a while, I realized I couldn't quite pull this off.

Tammy Staudt
Qigong Professor at NUNM

What was clear right from the very beginning is Dylan had this incredible yearning to be connected to what he then called God—creator energy, whatever you want to call this presence in the universe.

He had this exquisitely deep yearning, and he knew that's why he was here and what he wanted more than anything in life. Not only that, but he felt he was meant to serve that in some way, connecting to that and bringing that energy into the world. And it's been an underlying focus for him, truth for him, commitment for him, desire for him...

[It was] also an area where his own internal criticism can kick up the most—in his judgment of how he's succeeding with that or not.

☙

Something that was, in many ways, the hardest thing to come to terms with was my sense of time. I imagine it's similar for all those who receive a terminal disease diagnosis. It was especially hard for me because I am such a dreamer. Making plans and strategies to reach them was a huge motivation for me to get up in the morning, to keep working toward my goals. I had my next ten- and twenty-year plans fully laid out. With such uncertainty around my future, I've felt very unmotivated to do anything. I ask myself, "What would it mean if I didn't have goals or plans?" I wrote this poem to help me process that feeling:

Tomorrow

Countless yesterdays sold off for the mind's tomorrow.

Longing for that tomorrow to bring me Home today.

Borrowing from tomorrow until it went broke.

Oh, how much you've carried for me tomorrow,

a hope that a day would come when I could love me,

love this Life.

Yet striving, clawing up the hill of my pain,

reaching to get just a glimpse of the Light stretching over me,

the sunrise of my soul always just seeming to be

a tomorrow away.

So, I've built towers, walls, stairs, and windows,

but the Light has yet to touch my face.

Here now, with no more energy to build.

Here now, without a tomorrow to reach for,

just me and my pain.

At least I am not alone.

Pain, please guide me Home,

today.

I had to let go of my external goals, my career choice of being a clinical doctor, and all that I thought I would build out in the world, like my future Aikido dojo. I was forced, or given the opportunity to, focus primarily on my internal aspirations of rooting out the demons of my self-loathing and self-worth. One of the most important things I have been able to do with my diagnosis is put it all into perspective. After I got my feet back on the ground, I started to intentionally find ways to frame my situation that served my higher purpose. I started calling this my "highway to Buddhahood."

I have studied Buddhism and many other Eastern religious systems throughout the years. I also learned to practice Vipassana meditation and did so for many years. Sit in meditation for a while, and you soon have many sensations screaming for your attention and tempting you to move your position, scratch your neck, or get up all ready to flee the restless-ness. Now, since I am basically dealing with those things all the time, my disease offers me the opportunity to practice constantly.

❧

Tammy Staudt
Qigong Professor at NUNM

The way he organized around [his trauma] and dealt with it as a young child was to start performing, which is normal. It's a perfectly legitimate and healthy response. So much of Dylan's early life, so much of his identity was wrapped around his performance. And he was highly successful, whether it was sports or academics or socially... For someone who was so developed and so present in their body and connected to nature and all things, the sudden shutdown of the external body—was a huge process for him.

We have our unique versions of that. There's a time when we find that the very thing driving us, on some level, is destroying us. It's wearing us out. It's a task that never ends—it really doesn't matter what we've accomplished. We start to see that, wow, it's never good enough. It doesn't matter. The things I said I wanted to do, even now that I'm doing them, there's something that says that's not good enough, too. There's always another hurdle. It's a driver that doesn't stop.

Vikki Voss
Dylan's mother

Dylan met a special man who said, "Dylan, you want to be healed? What's your relationship with your mother?"
He said, "Good."
So the man said, "Give her some of your fingernails and your hair and have her put them in a homemade doll and pray with it for healing."
Isn't that beautiful—the power of a mother's love?
I am crafty. I grabbed one of Dylan's old red all-star jackets and folded it around this doll to make a jacket. And then I used old toe socks he wore to make little pants. I just pinned it all together.
Dylan's hair is short now. When he was young, we'd try all these wild haircuts. He'd have it spiky short on one side and flipping over on the other. So, I cut the doll's hair like that. It's on my altar and receives my prayers.

Brandt Stickley
Professor of Chinese Medicine at NUNM

All healing is at least bi-directional, if not multi-directional.
Dylan's capacity to articulate his experience so exquisitely, grounded in a quality of faith in something that emanated from him and emerged from within him and was brought into the world in a real way, in a tangible way, in the face of something so viscerally gripping on someone's life...
It brings us to the wellsprings of spirituality itself. What does it mean to be alive?

What does it mean to not know and to be able to go into the not-knowing, embrace the not-knowing, the fear of that unknown? To move through it to a place where a glimmer of light emerges and then grows like dawn coming above the horizon—into a light that spreads to everyone it makes contact with...

I can't say enough that the presence of mind and the facility and the fluency and fluidity of Dylan's language, plus the capacity to hold this in its brutal quality and yet allow beauty to emerge from it organically, uncontrived and real, is the healing part of it.

☙

In reality, we all have the same opportunity, of course, but I'm more like held in a prison with only two rooms: the meditation room to practice equanimity with all my sensations, or the dungeon, where I suffer from my resistance to what is. (Alright, maybe there are three rooms since I have Netflix on my tablet and can choose to avoid the question if I want, as well.)

For example, I have had months of tinea infections on my face and head. It's a common fungal infection that took the practice up quite a few notches. The itch would get so intense, with nothing I could do about it in the moment. So, I started to utilize affirmations. When it would become unbearable, I would remind myself: Through this sensation, I am becoming my higher self. Through it, I am offered the highway to Buddhahood. It helped to keep me in—or many times, return me to—a perspective that served my liberation.

If I needed to shoot right through the intensity of a sensation that was pulling me into despair, I would say in my mind: This sensation is reminding me that I am alive. I am here to feel this. Behind those words is the intention to redirect the enormity of the feelings that assist my spiritual awakening.

Other times, I respond by crying. I am much more emotional now and give myself the freedom to accept what emotions arise and need to flow. Equanimity will only get you so far; there has been a lot of grieving for the loss of a different relationship to tomorrow.

For equanimity to be effective, it is crucial to be mindful of our habitual labeling of situations and sensations. I like the saying, "Pain is pain, suffering is optional." That is the power of equanimity. It can unlock us from the suffering that we choose to associate with our symptoms, disease prognosis, and life circumstances.

May we all feel the peace residing between craving and repulsion.

Ꮽ

Adam Dombrowski
Housemate and fellow graduate student at NUNM
I remember Dylan providing a cocoon of support for me, where he would tell me stories about him growing up and when he was five, ten years in the past—he really saw me and understood me, as he's been through that himself.

He would help me to feel what the paradox was, that it didn't just have to be one or the other. That I could feel both ways together. He would see this conflict... "[There are] two sides of you playing tug of war, but maybe we don't have to play tug of war. Maybe we can build something together with these two sides of you."

He had plenty of mic-drop moments like that. Those perspective shifts really helped me to gain a healthy perspective and stop feeling so much friction from moment to moment.

Patrick Shanahan
Dylan's uncle
Once he had this disease and it was deeply progressing, I told him that my prayer every day for him is that he experiences a level of spirituality that none of us will ever experience. My Prayer was, please, God, give Dylan a spiritual experience that none of us will ever understand.

I was amazed at how productive he was without his physicality. While most victims lay on a bed and slowly die, he was not slowly dying; he was still living. He was still enjoying Seahawks games and Trail Blazers games. I would get text messages from him that were just fully engaged in life. I didn't realize that one could live at this level as an ALS patient.

And it doesn't have to be ALS, you know. You could go through hardships in your life and just never forget what Dylan was doing with ALS. If he's doing that with ALS, what can you and I do with our circumstances?

Dylan in Japan

A Violent Blossoming

How you tear at the threads of my skin.

It is like an itch, a cough so intense I'll burst at the seams,

a gag that will vomit me inside out.

Is that the nature of spring?

To open again to the world.

A violent blossoming,

exploding out into the surroundings with the seeds of life.

Our only difference, oh purple flowering tree of nature's royalty,

is I hesitate.

CHAPTER NINE

Still Unfixed

In November 2019, I had some rather odd treatment—an injection of Botox right into the salivary glands, specifically the parotid and submandibular glands. When my neurologist first told me about this option for managing saliva, I scoffed at the idea. But one of the silver linings of having such a serious illness is that I get to have a huge support team full of so many amazing people who brighten my days and make even the strangest scenarios possible.

I've got to start with my mother, for what love is closer to the love of the creator than that of a mother for her children? My mom moved in with me in August of 2018 and became my main support since the beginning of 2019. She has earned angelic status for the sacrifices she has made to help me.

Then, in no particular order:

My neurologist, Dr. Goslin, is a leading authority with ALS and is highly respected in the field. We have developed quite a warm and close relationship since we started together. Her whole team and staff are very compassionate.

Dylan and his mom Vikki

My pulmonologist, Dr. Libby, only works with ALS patients and would otherwise retire, but he is committed to our community. The same can be said for Dr. Goslin.

I have a dietitian that I don't see often since we studied quite a bit of nutrition in the naturopathic program.

I have a respiratory therapist who runs tests to evaluate my breath capacity—a very important marker—a couple of times a year.

My ALS society case worker, Cassie, is really sweet. She is a point person for all sorts of questions and coordinates everything from us getting things from the loan closet to addressing our various needs. We currently have a commode, an alarm button that I use in bed to call for help, and a Hoyer lift on loan thanks to her help.

I have the best augmentative communication specialist ever, Trinity. This is the device that I use to communicate, stay connected to loved ones through my phone and email, become a writer, and more. But it gets bumped and bent frequently. Trinity is a lifesaver, adjusting it so the camera will pick up my eyes again and keep me connected to the outside world.

My wheelchair pit team is important, considering I am in the chair all day. From the manager Tim to the two technicians, Bert and Rodney, they keep me moving in as much comfort as possible. Say no to pressure sores!

I have an occupational therapist, Nicole, and a physical therapist, Jackie, who divide and conquer my physical therapy for my upper body and lower half, respectively. They both come through home health. A few other nurses have come out for various things through home health as well. Darren comes out to do Asian bodywork, and Andrew does some massage therapy.

I also have a care team from my school of classical Chinese medicine, and I return to our student clinic to get acupuncture and the various other modalities that are employed there. They are like modern sages. I am blessed to have been able to study with such masters and continue to count my blessings that I can be treated by them.

Dr. Lee is a Korean Buddha and specializes in Chinese herbs.

Dr. Stickley is a magician with needles. He can see into the dark of my soul, yet still holds me with unconditional positive regard.

Dr. Silver and Dr. Quinn both specialize in a Japanese form of Chinese medicine. They have incredibly sensitive palpation skills. Commonly, the form uses contact needling with dull metal rods that don't break the skin, and small rhythmic burning of mugwort on the skin, a type of moxibustion. Their teacher in Japan, Dr. Bear, treats me when he is here teaching seminars.

Dr. Staudt is one of the most amazing people I have gotten to know in my life. Working and walking with her through this journey is something that brings me tears of gratitude. She was one of my Qi Gong instructors in the Chinese medicine program. It is hard to describe the healing work she does with brevity; suffice it to say that she is helping me stand more authentically in my human spirit.

That is quite a coalition. It is hard to imagine being back in my mom's house where I grew up, even though it is beautiful there. My sister, Willow, and my brother-in-law, Justin, come down from Olympia, Washington, as much as they can and have been a big help in many ways. My hometown, Shelton, has had a few fundraisers for me, and Willow and Justin have done a lot of organizing for them.

The Hama Hama oyster company, run by family friends Adam and Lisa James—Justin works there as well—has put on two awesome polar plunge events to fundraise for me. At the turn of the new year, the participants jump into the Hood Canal, a finger of the Puget sound.

My friends here in Portland have been an ongoing source of support. They put on a successful fundraiser for me online and a meal train sign-up, where people would bring meals for my mom and me. It finished a few months before I had feeding tube surgery. It was a real treat to be able to eat that well and have such delicious food before I couldn't taste anything anymore.

It is amazing how much can change about what one thought they wouldn't do, or thought they were incapable of doing.

☙

Tammy Staudt
Qigong Professor at NUNM

I remember early on in Dylan's process, he shared a song, Touch, with a group of us. It was the most magnificent refrain about reaching up a finger, touching the hand of God. Dylan shared it with the group, and they asked for it over and over. The whole group would sing the refrain with him. And it carried such divine energy and touched people so deeply. That song, in some ways, exemplified who he is:

Touch

Michelangelo's hand reaches out to God, God's hand reaches back

In a moment there is contact

What does God feel?

Exactly what I do when I touch you

Touch affirms reality with the experience of sensation

Neither to be clung to nor rejected

Life's intent is to be accepted

Happiness shared with the contact of Love

Can you feel it?

The air in your lungs, the fibers against your skin

The image of a smiling Buddha sitting with a grin

There connected between neurons, felt with a thought without sin

I hold on to it

Then let it go

So that my hands are free to help you feel your glow

I am an eye through which Light shines through

Until it touches you

And then two becomes One

With the union of earth and sun

Michelangelo's hand reaches out to God, God's hand reaches back

In a moment there is contact

What does God feel?

Exactly what I do when I touch you

What one does not see and feel can be said to be unreal

When we touch, we feel

The more we touch, the more we feel

The more we feel, the more our awareness will reveal

Then the unreal, will be uncovered from the veil

Of our ignorance, our suffering

So, touch this moment

From the heart to the heart

Breathing, Each Other, this World

Michelangelo's hand reaches out to God, God's hand reaches back

In a moment there is contact

What does God feel?

Exactly what I do when I touch you

Tammy Staudt, cont'd

What was interesting to watch is how deeply it moved people and how much they wanted that and could tune into their own heavenly nature or light in this connection through song—and yet it wasn't right. You know, his voice wasn't strong enough, or there'd be some other immediate criticism. We'd all see the gift, but [that criticism] didn't allow him to receive it, to really acknowledge and feel the profound impact of whatever comes through him has on people.

Christian Hoerr
Dylan's NA sponsor

He was so saturated with so many things to do...he always had some project. I remember he got this truck together that he wanted to resurrect to run it on biodiesel and all that stuff. And he did it, too.

It's just that the self-care piece, like that really deep internal work, kind of falls by the wayside. Part of working the steps is to dig into the root causes of some of those addictions, and it's supposed to be group therapy or like, mentored

self-therapy, where you're asking these questions of yourself in a fairly rigid structure in order to explore your motivations. And so often, for people who have self-destructive tendencies, it's like self-care comes to last. That's almost all of it, really.

But then he graduated from Evergreen, and that's when he left for Japan to pursue Aikido as a main mission while he taught school. He really got into Aikido—a blend of both a spiritual practice and a physical practice. And that was what harmonized things for him.

Brandt Stickley
Professor of Chinese Medicine at NUNM

I have to follow Dylan in being able to directly face the potential of failure in a therapeutic encounter. I must face the potential of it failing, so to speak, in this one realm.

It's an impetus to be humble... Dylan has issued a reminder of the spiritual power of humility. He is showing us the capacity to hold what can only be called a non-dual perception that is literally on the razor's edge between life and death itself, holding both as two poles of one reality.

It's real. It's as real as it gets, and it's as profound as it can be.

I would say Dylan's direct, perceptive communication and my navigation of the different roles that I've had... from teacher to mentor to practitioner to friend to colleague... the way that it's affected me is that I've had to surrender a holdover "salvationist heroic" perception of the role of a doctor, of a physician. That somehow there's this one thing that's going to [work]... That kind of thinking is not the same awareness of gray that Dylan's showing us.

The heroic or salvationist attitude must be surrendered to ever get to the truth of healing and to recognize that the final stages are independent of the physician always and are the purview and responsibility of the patient.

∽

Another member of my team, in a very different way, is Kimberly Warner, who approached me about her documentary about chronic illness, entitled Unfixed. Working with her on this project makes me feel we must have been friends in other timelines and we're reuniting to collaborate again. The film spotlights individuals living with chronic, or in my case terminal, illness and reveals the deeper truth: unfixed isn't good or bad. Sure, it's not fixed, but it's also not broken. Rather, we have come to accept an aspect of the reality of human experience by identifying as one who is unfixed. We have released the illusion that doctors can give us pharmaceutical solutions—as one might get for, say, high blood pressure—for our conditions.

Did you know that ninety percent of hypertension is idiopathic, meaning they don't know what caused the blood pressure to be elevated? If one doesn't understand the cause of something, it would follow that there is little chance of fixing the unknown cause. There is a time and place for everything, so sometimes drugs are important to reduce risks. My point is: common thinking is that problems are fixed, whereas the medical term controlled is more accurate. But the Unfixed community isn't offered the Kool-Aid of the illusion that things are getting fixed or that the cause of a symptom has been cured.

What would it even mean to be fixed? We are multidimensional beings, with physiology, thoughts, feelings, subtle energy pathways, and maybe even karmic influences. Who's to say actual causation doesn't incorporate past life experiences, too? My point is, we don't know. The medical community doesn't actually know.

It's likely if some in the Unfixed community had instead received a diagnosis that could be treated or pharmaceutically controlled, we might have gone back to sleep in the life patterns, attitudes, habits, or relationships that were contributing or even causing the symptoms that presented in the first place.

I think of the root cause of disease and suffering as interlinked. As the Buddha taught, the root of suffering is the ignorance of self. We are all Unfixed while we still experience the world through the veils of our illusions.

A fixed state of mind is rigid, but an unfixed life is fluid and more resilient, renegotiating what it means to live fully. Embracing the identity of Unfixed creates access to possibilities that the majority of society would dissuade us from.

We are all Unfixed, but only some of us accept that.

We are Unfixed while we still don't have unconditional love for our own unique brilliance.

We are Unfixed while we still can't see the inherent value and feel familial compassion for everyone we pass on the street.

We are Unfixed until it would hurt too much not to have the beauty of the natural world close and enveloping us.

We are Unfixed while we are still unaware that our bodies are ripe with the rivers of star dust, and our souls an outpouring from the hand of the divine source.

When I embody all of that, then I will be Fixed.

Until then, I'm a work in progress.

Dylan with Unfixed film crew

On One Knee

We may fall.

We might have mistaken our true calling.

How is one to know,

in the separation of our fear?

How could the Light of such Grace

be my birthright?

How could the mud and slime,

stagnating the flow of blood in my heart,

be the resonance of the Sun?

One who acts such as I,

who has hurt others,

lied to many,

none more important than to myself,

how could a sinner such as I begin

to knock on the door of Your Salvation?

What confidence to whisper Your Name

could come from such a soul?

Loneliness beckons me,

fear of never seeing Your Face,

never hearing Your Name called back to me

as my own.

Where else could I ever call home?

I must then knock,

but on one knee.

CHAPTER TEN

Sunrise From an Ambulance

It is 6:30 in the morning and, riding on a gurney in the back of an ambulance, I have quite a view of the sunrise projected against the clouds above, just visible through the back window. Admiring the array of oranges, pinks, and purples, I smile. This view is only available to me because of my orientation to the rear as we travel west on the highway, going back to my apartment after a night in the emergency room...

This was in April 2020, and I was accompanied by Sarah, a tall slender young woman of few words, and David, a seasoned EMT and cheerful, robust man. Do not let Sarah's lack of verbal engagement fool you—she engaged from within, with a keen eye and a quiet mouth, as I observed her notify David right away that he was pulling my breathing machine tubing while he was loading me into the ambulance. She didn't know most of the nurses on shift that night like David did, and it wasn't her nature to be chatty. And let's be honest, you don't need both of your EMT drivers to be telling jokes. They were a good team.

At about twelve that night, I had decided I needed help. I had been struggling to breathe for about an hour and wasn't showing any signs of improvement. My neck was one of the last parts of my body that I could move, so I called for my mom by rolling my head into a call button that sets off an alarm in her room. She was quick to understand that I was in distress because of the way my whole body was gasping for air. She asked what we should do, but since I couldn't talk and didn't have my eye-tracking communication device set up in my bedroom, I needed to spell out my answer with an alphabet card.

We tried the cough assist machine a couple of times. Because I am too weak to move enough air to clear my airways, it basically mimics a normal cough by forcefully sucking air out of my lungs and then pumping air back in. It is rather intense, but it can usually help dislodge mucus from my airways. Not this time. So, we were left with no other option than to call 911.

Fortunately, the fire department was just across the street from our apartment, so they arrived in no time. They took my vitals and found that my oxygen saturation was much below normal. It is a funny thing to need technology to prove the obvious: I was suffocating.

As a doctor, I understand, of course, the usefulness of getting a baseline to assess treatment. But in the moment, I'd skip that step to get me breathing first.

When they got me on oxygen, I calmed down a little and my oxygen saturation came up to low normal. I was still having difficulty breathing, and whatever was obstructing my airway was still there. The EMT expressed the concern that as soon as they took me off the oxygen, my numbers would return to worrisome levels. It was clear that I needed to go to the hospital.

They slid me out of bed directly onto the gurney and loaded me into the ambulance. On the way to the emergency department, they gave me a cocktail of bronchodilators through a vaporizing machine called a nebulizer. Upon arriving at the hospital, they ran a bunch of tests: chest x-ray to check for pneumonia, blood work looking for infection, and even a pulmonary angiogram to check for a pulmonary embolism. It took three hours of exceedingly difficult breathing and feelings of suffocation before I finally began to breathe easily again.

It took a few more hours for the results of all the tests to come back negative. They settled on a diagnosis of a mucus plug that must have resolved after the bronchodilators created enough space in my airways for the plug to clear. Then Sarah and David loaded me and my ventilator back on a gurney to be transported home.

And so, we have come full circle in the story, where I am being driven west on the highway, looking out the rear window of the ambulance, soaking up the sunrise with an ear-to-ear grin, feeling blissed out as each full, unrestricted breath moved in and out.

Through the process of ALS, I have been stripped of innumerable aspects of my previous life. I'm down to the most basic of pleasures and elements of gratitude: breathing, my communication device, and my friends and family who can share in my love of life. Life can be that simple. Happiness can be that simple.

My circumstances have forced me, in a large way, to orient myself to the rear window. If we are always looking through the front window of the car of our lives— towards the longings we hope the future will fulfill—we tend to miss the opportunity to appreciate what we already have.

There is nothing wrong with looking to the future to ask for more. It is the nature of our longing to be ever reaching for a greater understanding of our environment and ourselves, to discover new technologies that further simplify our means of survival, and to purify the expression of the soul through the arts. Just know that, like the expansion of the universe through infinite space, our desires are similarly unlimited. As soon as one is fulfilled, there are ten more to fill its place. It will never be complete. Therefore, it is wise to seek a balance between our ever-expanding desires and our appreciation of what we see through the rear view.

Rumi Meets Huangdi: Inspiring Meditation

Tilting our inner ear to the fire,

resonating out both ends of the candle's Light;

within, without, and all about.

Listening for the guiding Light of truth,

in all its totality.

On that day,

how easily excited it will be to rise from slumber,

maybe even being inclined to help the sun,

were our place not to rise together.

How joyous the moment will be

when that outward-looking fire of awareness

reunites with that inner longing of water's resting place,

on inward-reflecting pools of desire to be whole.

What voice do you use to talk to such a one?

What title would you use to reference it,

if every day could be one with a Beloved?

Would that change your tone or color of the day?

For in the sun rays would not only be the warming of skin,

but also the guiding vector back within.

How long can you hold the Light of attention to burn through, to where the fire meets the other side of the wax tunnel?

Now is the time to come home to our inner Source,

where looked and looker meet.

One eye/I for both,

and both for my Beloved.

Dedicated to Heiner Fruehauf and the NUNM CCM Faculty, 2017

CHAPTER ELEVEN

Trach in the Time of Pandemic

Letter to Dr. Messinger
ND who treated Dylan in his early stages of ALS

Hello Dr. Messinger,

First, I would like you to know how apologetic I am for not getting back to you for so long. I am still alive and doing well. I hope you will understand when I explain how I have been feeling.

I had stopped seeking treatment for ALS, and in many ways surrendered to the progression. Some of it was the time and money involved with the treatments, but a larger part was the loss of hope. Hope is a tricky thing with terminal illnesses. I had to believe in the treatment we were doing. It required me to put some of myself out there in hopes that this treatment would be successful. I believe in the power of our expectations. So I expected to get better. That is why I didn't do the voice banking when I had the chance because I expected to get better before it would come to that.

I first started to see this change in a family member. I would tell them about the new treatment I was doing and the reasons I believed it would be effective, but I could tell they were guarded against my optimism. I figured they felt it was safer not to hope, to avoid the disappointment of the world not meeting their expectations. I could understand that strategy, and would eventually know it through experience.

So, it was hard to come to terms with that change in myself. I always intended to reply to your email. It has been in my inbox to remind me. Although with my varying degrees of engagement with the world, it has gotten buried under the times when I would not check email. It has been difficult for me at times. I hope you know I am super grateful for the work we did together, and I am not trying to provide any indictment against you. I just couldn't start over with a new person, my mom was burnt out, and eventually, I fell into a self-protection mechanism to guard against disappointment.

I've still been working with Dr. Staudt on energetic and soul healing. I completely believe that full union with my Maker unleashes infinite healing potential. If it is of the plan, I will rise again to my feet, and if I need these experiences with ALS for my soul to evolve as needed in this life, so be it. I can only go with the flow.

So, I am still healing on the inside, but my nerves have continued to die. I got a tracheostomy on March 25th. It has been quite an adjustment. If my super-power is in this process, it would surely be adaptability. It is pretty smooth now. I have normalized to the intensity of sensations that come with the trach getting moved around with transfers and such. There are clear benefits, of course. Being able to suction into my lungs is a game-changer. The last two weeks I have had a minor URI, and I would surely have been hospitalized without the trach. So, it keeps me alive.

I have a strong sense of purpose since I have been writing a lot for my website that I recently launched, alongside my mission to become a fully Self-realized human embodiment of the Creator. LifeBreath.net

Feel free to pass along to anyone you think might be interested.

Enough about me, how is Southern Oregon? The pictures you sent are beautiful, thanks. It must be nice to spread out in the country on your ranch. How is your clinic? It is surely a different clinical environment during the pandemic here in Portland.

Well, I am happy to reconnect with you. I hope this finds you in good spirits and health.

Much love,

Dylan

☙

When COVID happened, I started thinking about being proactive and getting the tracheostomy sooner rather than later. With ALS, any respiratory infection can be life-threatening due to the risks of respiratory crisis, which could result in an emergency tracheostomy. You can imagine, then, how unsettling the COVID-19 pandemic was for folks like me, especially before the vaccine came through. Social distancing was not an issue for me since it was quite risky to be out and have one of my saliva aspiration episodes. It could take hours to get the mucus out, and I really needed to be home with all my equipment to manage it.

The surgery had been recommended by my pulmonologist and neurologist many months before. As I mentioned before, I had decided to get it done at some point because it could increase life expectancy, but I had no idea how to decide when to get such a life-changing invasive procedure. It is hard for me to put into words how this weighed on me.

My doctors had informed me about clear timing markers for surgery, like becoming short of breath without the non-invasive ventilation mask, or if my oxygen saturation became chronically depressed, etc.—none of which applied to me. I was managing, which left me in a grey area. How would I choose to put a tube into my lungs and become completely dependent on the ventilation machine to breathe?

The indecision was overwhelming, and I needed space from it. I went into periods of hibernation, not checking emails or returning any texts. The stories in movies provided the temporary solace I needed.

Eventually, I started to fill in the gaps of the great unknown surrounding the surgery. I researched the common complications from the surgery and the daily maintenance it would require. I got a list of questions ready for my phone consult with my pulmonologist. I sought out counsel from my most trusted advisors. One, who I deeply respect, hit home when they explained that it made a lot of sense to get the surgery soon, to mitigate the risk of getting infected with the coronavirus. Emotions aside, it started to sink in that it was time.

The coronavirus situation was a serious factor. Many people who get COVID, especially those who do not have a strong immune system, develop pneumonia, where part of the lungs fill with fluid. It could be life-threatening if I got infected, but I'm much better equipped to deal with it with a trach. The direct suctioning of my lungs is a game changer, and it is a closed system, therefore less chance of infection.

Another bonus of the surgery was I could stop wearing a ventilation mask, which would open up my face to smile.

I let my pulmonologist know at our next phone appointment I was considering getting the surgery. It was a huge step for me to tell him I was considering it, but he raised the ante and added a new layer of complexity. He thought that hospitals might be over capacity soon and would no longer allow elective surgeries. Because I was not in a respiratory crisis, my surgery would be considered elective. He recommended that if I wanted it soon, I should get the surgery that week. Otherwise, I could have to wait months until the coronavirus situation improved substantially.

It was impossible for me to shift gears that quickly, but by Friday I called to tell him I was ready to go ahead with it the next week.

Arriving in the surgery lobby was eerie. There was nobody behind the desks to check me in, and there were no other patients in the huge, empty room. It was a ghost town. The surgery went well, but normally I would have been sent to a different post-operative recovery area of the hospital once I stabilized. Now they were keeping that side of the hospital separate for COVID patients, leaving me in the ICU for eight days with a strict policy of only one visitor for my entire stay so they could limit exposure risks of the coronavirus.

But here I am.

I've made it to the other side.

Now you can see me smile.

Dylan post-tracheostomy

PART III:

Undoing

The Resurrection of Fall

Crimson colors of autumn like the flames of purgatory,

stripping us down to the bare-naked branches of youth

where we stand before the mirror of ourselves, itself.

Our life flashing before our eyes, instantaneously,

we understand the fallacy of our ways.

The sapling blossoms in the dying seed

to return to the original image.

Wind carries the leaves of outgrown consciousness

like a snake sheds its skin.

The flames of transformation, red, orange, and yellow,

the resurrection of fall.

CHAPTER TWELVE
In the Midst

I have loved to smile at people for as long as I have been me. It is instinctual. If I think about it, it aligns with the base of my life perspective. I smile at a friendly world, and I see a friendly world smile back at me. I especially enjoy smiling at people in my current state, when they might assume I have more to frown about than smile. My smile has more impact with the element of surprise.

All of that has been the context for me noticing the loss of mobility on the right side of my face: I'm starting to have a one-sided smile. I cannot imagine not being able to make facial expressions. It's such an integral part of nonverbal communication, and I am already nonverbal.

Now that I have a tube in my throat, it is harder to swallow. The saliva that does go down my throat ends up in my lungs. This means I am more dependent on getting suction to clear my lungs. I don't mind that as much since the other way my saliva goes is onto my face.

I look like I have rabies. Luckily, I have been in quarantine, and I have not been around people except when I go to the hospital for my health care needs. When I do, I like wearing a mask. Even though it is pointless

Dylan and friend Erin Griffen

for me because I don't breathe through my mouth or nose, it does hide my drool.

I have passing thoughts that it makes me look more disabled or more "out of it." It doesn't matter though. Ultimately, I come back to my favorite phrase: What you think of me is none of my business. It reinforces the need to love myself as I am, regardless of cultural norms about drool or anything else.

There have been ten thousand things that I couldn't imagine living with along this journey, but here I am. My whole external life has completely changed.

I've moved to an adult family home for people with tracheostomies. There are only a few in Oregon, and they were all full. This necessitated that I move to a place in Vancouver, WA, across the river. It would be not much more than a thirty-minute drive from my old apartment in Portland, but it was like moving to a foreign country, considering how complicated it was to switch from Oregon Medicaid to Washington Medicaid.

My survival is dependent on Medicaid. The machines that keep me alive, my wheelchair, my communication device, and all their maintenance are incredibly expensive. Not to mention that I require very specialized care. Needless to say, my relationship to health insurance is very unique—yet I had to move to establish residency before I could find out if I qualified for WA Medicaid. Talk about a trust fall.

Practically speaking, I can't move anywhere else. There are no other group homes with availability in Washington state, and I can't imagine switching back to Oregon Medicaid. I don't have an option of living with family, because I require too much care. So, I plan on making the best of it here.

This does change my outlook on life. My fatalistic voice would say I am stuck. That voice, although not positive, does get the gist of it.

I had such a complete healthcare team before I moved. For example, my pulmonologist gave me his cell number so I could text him with any questions, recognizing the difficulty for me to call his office. Intermixed with our discussions about my health was our outlook for the Blazers' prospects for the upcoming season. Having gaps in my team leaves me feeling incomplete and more insecure without those people to turn to in times of need.

The other way to look at it is: that the increased need for caregivers in my safety net has caused me to be less trusting.

It is not exactly trust—more about needing more assurances and carefully designed systems.

It has taken a while to get a system in place here, with a lot of new staff. I'm double-checking with the owners frequently to make sure the system is implemented and new staff is receiving the proper training. I would say I am more cautious when it comes to my safety net.

I guess it is about trust.

☙

Tammy Staudt
Qigong Professor at NUNM

There's this work that I do in the Shan Ren Dao system, which is looking at the emotional consciousness levels of healing. They call it Bing Xing, which are the deepest ingrained patterns and the hardest ones to shift. They are ingrained for generations, throughout humanity. Each one of those is a lot of work to reach to that acceptance. I am inspired by his ability to recognize resistance, to see what's there and to come into a radical self-acknowledgment and responsibility and opportunity of what this means and what the reflection is and what it might be pointing to. Dylan's capacity—to see possibility and opportunity rather than clinging to what was is—has remarkable to watch. Would that I had his capacity, courage, and grace...

☙

The other area that changed drastically in the last quarter of 2020 is my health. Besides the progression of ALS, I have had a urinary infection, pneumonia, and a very serious undiagnosed gastrointestinal issue. I had an abdominal CT scan, but I am still waiting for a referral to a gastrointestinal doctor in WA, and I don't have anyone to do a thorough evaluation. In the meantime, my heart rate occasionally spikes following meals. When my heart rate accelerates, my oxygen consumption increases. My breath volume is standardized by the ventilator, so my only option is to breathe faster. That has limits, and I can be left feeling like I can't quite get enough air with each breath. This will go on for hours until my heart rate slows down. It has affected my engagement level, leaving me to try to distract myself from the constant thought that I need more air.

My legs have also become much weaker. I used to use my legs to push a secondary alarm to call for help if my communication device crashed, which it does occasionally. Secondary alarm systems necessitate body movement, but I have run out of moving parts. This is a huge challenge to my safety and well-being, and it makes me even more dependent on my caregivers.

I have begun to shift from thinking I would live forever, to maybe not-so-long, with a terminal disease that has no cure. Don't get me wrong. I believe in miracles and that whatever can be done can be undone. It just got me thinking, if my time is short on this earth, I don't want to spend it fussing or fighting.

In light of that realization, there is no relationship that is not worth an attempt at saving. If this is the last time I see this person, what feeling do I want to share with them before I go?

I don't have a lot of pleasures left to enjoy from before, so the people in my life are that much more important to me. I understand this is rather cliché, but it is so true: with great loss, you can really learn to appreciate what you have left.

No Sign of Life

Still no sign of Life

I have been searching relentlessly,

looking under every rock and stone

dipped into each alley and

stared into the black box only to see myself on the other side.

This is a barren wasteland.

No altars to sit at.

Nothing

Just an empty plate with only the memory of the foods of past.

Muffled screaming out into the oncoming gusts of air.

The storm grows into Stillness,

violently beating itself into submissive surrender,

and sweet satisfaction.

There is nowhere to go, nothing to do, and nothing to remember.

Selfless sleep,

daylong daydreams looking out of closed eyes.

At the silent stirrings,

the Spark

in all space

in no time

the flame stops, coils, sways, dematerializes into sparkling dust

glowing throughout this

Emptiness

CHAPTER THIRTEEN

The Deep Dark Woods

Christian Hoerr
Dylan's NA sponsor

Working with Dylan was always a joy, but I wasn't just his sponsor. I was a mentor to him, but I think that was a much smaller part of our relationship. When he started to talk to me about sponsorship, he told me he was living in the woods in a tent. I told him there was a cabin on my property, nobody was living there, and it needed a little work. I offered a work trade and told him, "You can't do school and live in a tent. That's ridiculous. All your books would turn to mold."

I started out with like, "Look, here, here's shelter, no questions asked. Everyone should have that." But I just wanted to start there. Like, you need some firewood, and you don't have a truck? Well, here, borrow mine for the day. I didn't hold those things over him like we had a contract... I was a little young to be a dad, but if I'd had children very young, Dylan could be my son. I wanted there to be somebody like that for him. 'This is the way to act in the world.'

He always had such an awesome attitude about contributing and being part of the community and helping out. He was focused and disciplined during that time. He was able to white-knuckle his decision [not to use marijuana] and say, "I'm not doing that, because it interferes with me, and I have this example of this person that I'm living with who shows me that it can be done."

We idolize redemption arcs, right? We idolize, you know, the power from the rags to riches. And here it is. Dylan is what it really looks like.

…this is this person who came from the most humiliating and awful abuse. And like him, he left that behind to find what it meant to be a kind person, a loving person. And in the midst of all these other toxic masculine messages, he found what matters.

How we relate to others is the most important thing. And he shows us that.

And he has a different message for our society, one that's not about conquering it. There's no more territory left to conquer. We're done with that phase of expansionism. It's time to stop focusing on outer space and focus on inner space.

Patrick Shanahan
Dylan's uncle

In some ways, one of those things he may have inherited from the Shanahan genes is the trait to keep fighting and pushing and never giving up. My brother Bill took that and spun it in a very negative way. Dylan took that same trait and spun it in a very positive way. He never went into that negative zone that his father did.

Vikki Voss
Dylan's mother

For some reason, his dad chose Dylan. He saw that Dylan was special… There was hair pulling, dragging. And other times it was this walking on eggshells. You know, when you talk about mental abuse? I just didn't know when he was going to explode. He was always kind of in a bad mood. The kids didn't necessarily want to bring their friends home. At basketball games, he would yell at

Willow, and when they were watching the tape on Monday, the coach would turn the volume off because it was so embarrassing to hear him.

[Shan's] father was very physical and crazy too. You had to be home, and if you're two seconds late... Shan played guitar, and we would sing. We'd go on hikes, have nights in the woods, adventures. But his moods would spoil it too.

Willow Shanahan
Dylan's sister

You know how Morningstar [Dylan's dog] died? Oh, it's not a good story. I mean, it helps you understand Dylan and my dad's relationship. Dylan had a dog, Morningstar, who wasn't the best behaved. It wasn't the nicest dog. It loved Dylan.

When I graduated from college and came home, our parents went to Africa to teach. They didn't want to sell the magical schoolhouse on Harstein Island, so I said that I would watch the house, and moved in. Around that same time, Dylan was starting his adventure trip to Japan to teach English, and he wanted to leave the dog at the schoolhouse.

So now I've got my parents' dog, Luna; Dylan's dog, Morningstar; and then my mom had gotten me a puppy. It was kind of crazy. And Luna and Morningstar didn't really get along. Then our dad moves home—he's kind of done with Africa—and he takes over watching Morningstar, and I move out.

He doesn't like Morningstar. Even though his dog Luna was equally bad, he's done taking care of this dog and wants Dylan to find another home for it. I think Morningstar nipped at the UPS person's heels, and my dad was like, "It needs to be put down. This is a mean dog, it bites people." He told Dylan, "You better find another home or I'm killing your dog." But Dylan was in Japan.

I told my dad on the phone, "Don't kill Dylan's dog. Your relationship is already rocky. There's no coming back if you kill Dylan's dog."

He's like, "I already dug the hole." That was his answer.

I feel like I'm making this story up because it's so crazy, but that was the way he was—so spiritual and in love with human rights and all this, then weird about other things.

My husband has a good way of putting it: "Bill Shanahan wants peace so much, he'll punch you in the face for it."

Shanahan family portrait

The Toxic Masculine

Bitch ass crybaby

You weak wimpy excuse for a man

Suck it up, toughen up

You're an embarrassment to the Shanahans

What are you doing sitting up in the trees crying

Get on the ground and get to work, you're not dying

So carry your weight and stop whining

They're going to pick you apart

if you keep being such a pussy

Work hard, eventually you'll see

Bitch ass crybaby

Stop singing songs and be strong

Stop your dancing and prancing

They're going to say you're gay

Bitch ass crybaby

Don't tell me about your feelings

Push through

Nobody cares about your shit

So sit down and work on your penmanship

Bitch ass crybaby

Life's not fair, so don't stare

Pick up a shovel and dig a hole, deep

Lay in there and weep

Stay until your innocence is dead

Then you can finally think with your head

Bitch ass crybaby

Lift up your chin, don't forget to grin, make sure you win

Lift up your chin, don't forget to grin, make sure you win

Lift up your chin, don't forget to grin, make sure you win

ᘏ

Vikki Voss
Dylan's mother

When Dylan was going to Evergreen, he was in counseling. He got to this point, "Why did my mother put me through that? Why didn't she leave him?" You know, if someone hurts your child, you remove them from that situation. I see now that he is right. A child should never be scared to that level of terror. I'm just so forgiving. It's part of my nature. "Okay, it'll be different this time."

Dylan would say, "How can you forgive him?" He had cut him off. But then later, when [Shan] had the stroke, Dylan changed that. He was trying to help him.

Mikael Brucker
Fellow graduate student at NUNM

We would rent out a cabin or a house somewhere and do our own informal Qi Gong retreat. We called ourselves Qi Bros. There was a continual thread and bond.

Adam Dombrowski
Housemate and fellow graduate student at NUNM

A few months after he received the diagnosis—I'm not sure exactly how far he was progressing—Donald, Mikael, Dylan, and I all spent a weekend at a cabin. We put on this one song by A Tribe Called Quest called "Can I Kick It?" One of our friends pulled out a ukulele, maybe it was, a guitar. He was playing the basic notes for that song, and we were just rapping the song and kind of doing the call and response of:

"Can I kick it? Yes, you can! Can I kick it? Yes, you can! And I'm gone!"

We were just the four of us at that moment, fully in the rhythm and the beat and the melody of the music, having this overjoyed moment together without giving a crap about what else is happening. About his diagnosis and what else we were stressing... it didn't matter. It was just about that love between the four of us.

Kimberly Warner
Director of Unfixed Media

I could feel their love for Dylan and their excitement for his life force on this planet. That was really dear to hear, especially as we're still living in a patriarchal society and men often don't get to share these deep levels of connection and honor and relationship together. There's just deep love there.

శ్వ

Circle of Qi

Translucent light with the early morning mist.

The full moon shines candlelight into our Qi Gong circle.

The monk in his robes and Columbia jacket

guides us through the bamboo staff technique.

The air is a sea of Qi as it spirals off my staff

like a paddle in the bay with trailing phosphorescent swirls.

The chill air on my bare hands is unnoticed,

while my focus is on my steaming breath.

While the moon descends behind a silhouetted tree,

casting its last reflected light,

I twist my staff and kick my leg with a strong exhale of release.

The light of the sun begins to crawl up the hill behind us.

I raise my staff over my head with a full breath of life.

Written at Thich Nhat Hanh's monastery and retreat center in France, 2006.

Dylan in his first few months of life

To Be Received

The momentum of love The power of movement.

Can build the pristine utopia And shatter the walls of hate.

Not the internalized hate,

Sitting motionless, rotting the soul.

Mental masturbation of slow suicide.

Somebody didn't love me like I needed

and I hate myself for it.

The self-proclaimed victimhood of betrayal.

Forgiveness lies in the eyes of the beholder.

Receiving forgiveness is to receive love.

Where shadow meets the light,

and is made whole.

A baby received in the womb,

the return of innocence.

Dedicated to Dr. Tamara Staudt

Something stirred in me after I watched a heartbreaking film about addiction. That combined with the work I have been doing with Dr. Tamara Staudt recently, I wrote this.

CHAPTER FOURTEEN

Loving My Attacker

On my worst days, a certain picture best represents me. The picture is of Morihei Ueshiba, the founder of Aikido, which can be translated as "the way to harmonize with the energy of the universe." I researched his life extensively when I first got into Aikido, and I came to understand that the creation of this art didn't come out of the air, but through a devotion to the higher path through real hardships. Having lived through World War II, he said, "Before the bomb, the battlefield was the warrior's way of life, but after, their way of life became the battlefield."

The utter challenge of those days summons in me this image, this spirit of harmony and resilience. As an aside, harmony is one of my favorite words. Harmonic resonance has so much subtle power behind it. It is a very real and powerful principle of the world: in 1940, the Tacoma Narrows Bridge experienced high winds that caused a resonance vortex, causing its collapse. With that same measure of power, we can choose what we want to resonate with, and how we will affect others, by setting our internal dialed-in frequency.

Our convictions are put to the test when safety is threatened by an attacker. The physiology of fear triggers an accelerated pulse, contraction of muscle tone, and sweat instantly beading up. How are we to respond? Do we heed the call of our instinctive animal nature to fight back, rebel, and attack the attacker, or flee the scene to make a great escape?

My tough moments can be compared to this attacker scenario, and a night in May 2020 was one of the worst. I wear boots at night to counter calf stiffness and hold my ankles in a neutral position. That night, my foot and the boot rolled off to one side, putting pressure on the side of my foot, and my help alarm malfunctioned, leaving me with no external options for relief. The pain grew so intense that it made my leg twitch. And I was alone, in the empty vacuum of space, left to deal with this attacker.

And the attacker was at me with full sensational force, from one in the morning until after five o'clock, as I worked on strengthening harmony with my inner source. It was a long training session. The feeling that nobody could help collapsed in on me. There's no helpline in the moment of truth. All I could do was react internally—recalling the brilliance of Jeff Haller's Aikido dojo's name, Inside Moves.

That night, part of me was in panic, even though I was relatively calm. I spent a lot of that time in meditation and prayer. Fluid had collected in my lungs, putting out a rumbling gargle with each exhale. It was not obstructing my breathing too much, though if it got worse, I knew it would set off the alarm on my ventilator and wake my mother up. Not to be masochistic, but I was almost hoping that would happen. I was willing to trade brief air hunger to end a seemingly endless battle with my attacker. At that point, all options were on the table.

Then the attacker brought a thorough combination move to my practice. It's worth noting that any effective attack brings about an element of shame, stimulating thoughts like Why me or What did I do to deserve this? But this attack was ruthless. I usually urinate once or twice a night, and that night was no different. Since I had no way of getting help, I could only hold back the floodgates for so long, until eventually, nature took its course. As Bob Marley sang, "Once a man, twice a child," but usually that second return to childhood comes much later. There is not much more humbling, as a forty-year-old man, than to have to lay in my own urine.

With O'Sensei's image nearby, I remembered his teachings that every attack has an opening. By attacking, there is always a weak spot, an angle of imbalance, or a vulnerability of the attacker. That is why Aikido is the path of invincibility: the one who does not fight can never be defeated.

❦

Tammy Staudt
Qigong Professor at NUNM

Watching his courageous acceptance of each level of this journey, this physical journey where each new taking away—in some ways, looking at it before you get there—has this sort of horror... [Especially when] we've been so capable in our body and assumed that we'll always be in our bodies.

...a year before [that] would have been horrifying, too embarrassing, too shameful, and yet each step of the way, he has courage and capacity to meet that with this deep self-acceptance. The body has forced him over and over into a deep acceptance of now, of 'who I am, despite how my body behaves.'

Adam Dombrowski
Housemate and fellow graduate student at NUNM

It was art and science. It was black and white, day and night. There's a world where we all recognize that living in the paradox of life is where harmony comes together, where yin and yang are in balance. And we can all have that contentment with life, even while we feel some tension or angst. That harmony, that balance, that dance of life.

❦

Because Aikido doesn't have any attacks, it can therefore always be in harmony with the powers of the universe. Similarly, O'Sensei teaches me to harmonize with my worst days—not to resist them, not to fight them, not to run away from them. Just as every attack has an opening, so too does every worst day have a lesson, an opportunity for growth. And although Aikido never attacks, it does teach us to always lead. We are guiding the attacker into the spiderweb of our benevolence, to dilute violence in the ocean of our compassion, diffusing the attack by utilizing its opening to guide us back to harmony.

It is much easier to focus on harmonizing with the rhythms of the universe when it is a sunny day in the park, but it takes a muddy swamp to grow a lotus flower, immense pressure to make a diamond, and rain to get a rainbow.

Mirroring this example, I practice Aikido by guiding my worst days into the context of my life's classroom for the evolution of my soul. I can choose to rise above my despair, fear response, shame, and sense of isolation and separation; to harmonize with my inner source, the creative power of the stars' formation.

When I practice holding those roots of my being, I'm not consumed by the attacks of circumstance. This allows me to uncover in my reactions where fear still grips my body and mind. They are then brought into the light of consciousness, where they melt, layer upon layer, one worst day at a time, until the full power of the sun has returned to the dawn of my rebirth, in this life or the next.

Dylan sitting outside at care facility

147

I Am the Mouth

I am the mouth of the Grand River of times unfolding.

My eyes blossom like roses, perfectly in their own time.

I swallow the seasons, digesting them to dust,

Burping up the aroma of bliss,

Carried on a warm breeze swirling a kiss,

On the forehead of those stuck in the cold of winter.

Sacrificing my body as the kindling's glowing warmth,

Golden rays melting the ice separating us.

As one, unified in symbiotic strength.

As one, singing the song of love.

What could there be to fear?

It all falls away, as the soul rises to meet the sun/son.

CHAPTER FIFTEEN

Brave New World

My dear friends visited recently. Nearly the whole time they were here, they rubbed my arms as we talked. We were connected physically and emotionally. Obviously, I can't rub their arm back. I can't give them a hug or anything like that. Does that mean I don't have the capacity to be intimate? Let me quote Luke Skywalker in Star Wars 8: "Reach out with your feelings." Through empathetic ability, I can still touch someone, so to speak. Isn't that the core of intimacy?

In two years, I went from not being able to use my right hand, to being on a ventilator and not being able to move my body. In another six months, I had to move into a state adult family home, without many visitors and no way to attend any social functions. I am with nurses and caregivers predominately and stay connected with my friends and family through text and email. All along the way, this has been incredibly, beyond measure, humbling, and was a demolition to my egotistical self-image and transformative to my intimate relationships.

This is where my freedom came from. I mean, What the fuck do I care what anyone thinks about me? I'm dying here. Life is short, so take care of the most important things first. We can talk about the weather later.

Dylan's 40th birthday pub gathering

Intimacy, then, boils down to making it apparent I love a person and am here to support them if needed.

My practice of intimacy became, as much as possible, complete presence with the people I am around. Feeling them with my empathy and intuition, but also using all my senses and deductive reasoning. Do I notice the light twitch of her mouth while she waits, suggesting potential anxiety? Do I hear the extra force in his voice saying that he might also be angry? Letting go of my projected self-image, and letting go of my desire to control what others think of me, they were replaced by a trust in others to accept my authentic self-expression. With that trust in others, an openness and vulnerability naturally filled me—the fertile soil from which intimacy blossoms.

I must remind myself that I enjoy the feeling of intimate interactions when my frequent fevers might suggest that I keep my distance. When we are sick, our immune cells release hormone-like chemicals, called cytokines, that alter our mood, to promote social isolation and limit the spread of disease. We "just want to be alone." People with chronic disease, like me, are at risk of being biochemically closed off and socially isolated for extended periods of time. Often, it takes conscious effort to override the body-mind when we are not feeling well, whether that is from chronic disease, headaches, menstrual cramps, or allergies.

But humans also have a primal desire to share love. Intimacy is the platform for us to give and receive love on all levels. Oxytocin is the hormone of love and bonding, playing a role in childbirth and serving as the antithesis to TNF-alpha and other cytokines—the stress hormones and neurotransmitters that would keep us apart.

There are ways—besides having a baby—we can increase our levels of oxytocin. The easiest is through physical contact. A reminder: ALS only affects motor nerves, so I can feel everything with my intact sensory nerves. I've made sure I am touched every day. Massage therapy is not covered by my insurance, but physical therapy is. All my caregivers are trained in my stretching routine. And because massage is such an important part of care and well-being, I pay out of pocket for one weekly. With severe symptoms, like a Crohn's disease flare-up, the body might be too sensitized to pain for a full-body rubdown. A perfect calming technique in those situations is a foot rub, which I love.

When I was first unable to move my body, I would wake up in the middle of the night feeling claustrophobic and stressed, unable to get back to sleep. If went on for long, I would ask my mom, who was taking care of me at the time, to rub my feet. It worked every time. My aunt Quyen gives me a foot massage every time she visits, and it is lovingly intimate. Rubbing the feet helps our energy descend and shifts our nervous system to a more parasympathetic state—an excellent remedy to stress, which causes our energy to go up and out.

It is important to point out that any time we experience physical or emotional pain, it is always paired with a stress response. Chronic illness is almost always accompanied by chronic stress, although usually not experienced consciously. Therefore, I recommend foot rubs to everyone, saving our stressed-out world one foot massage at a time.

Life is symbiotic. I am an extreme example of this, literally surviving on the kindness of others. I need assistance with daily life and am fully dependent on others for survival. I don't have a way to work. Although I am a writer, I don't have any income. So, the kindness of society, collectively deciding to provide healthcare for someone in my position, has provided coverage for all my doctors, my in-home healthcare, my wheelchair, my augmentative communication device, my formula of pureed food for my feeding tube, and my caregivers who give my mother a break eighty hours a week. That is a ton of financial support from taxpayers who decided that humanity would be benevolent—to me. As crazy as we might think the world is, my survival is a testament to the kindness in it.

If we look deep enough, we'll see that we are all dependent on each other to survive, whether that is due to someone else growing your food, building your home, raising you, or providing you with an education, transportation, and protection. Even the most self-sufficient person on the planet is dependent on plant life to breathe and eat.

Similarly, for being so dependent on so many people, mostly, I am alone.

Or am I?

If intimacy is our loving embrace with our heart of the "other," can I not always be in an intimate state of mind with the divine?

I'm not talking about some man in the clouds but of all existence.

The "Other."

Rumi's poetry exemplifies this most beautifully with their use of the "Beloved." That, for me, is the highest form of intimacy—extending to all of creation, all of life, and all our brothers and sisters of humanity. To hold the whole world with love, that is impartial intimacy.

એ

Roger Batchelor
Acupuncture professor at NUNM

There was a time right after COVID when my wife Janine and I both crash-landed on some land on the big island of Hawaii. I pulled out of my driveway in Newberg to fly there for spring break, and the governor of Oregon was closing down the state for the pandemic right as I was pulling out of the driveway. When I got to Hawaii, the governor shut down the state, all the beaches, etc. About two days later, my flights were canceled. I couldn't leave there for three and a half months. There wasn't a single commercial airline leaving anywhere in Hawaii.

The process bonded us. We bought some land and started camping on it. As we were clearing the land, hiring a bulldozer to put in a road and a water tank... It was a wonderful time in my life, and it turns out, he was sharing it from a distance! Dylan sent a text that said, "Dr. Batchelor"—I wish he could call me Roger— "I can feel your chi from here!"

Keep healing, Dylan. Because as you do, you heal so many people with you.

ও৹

When we are talking about concepts like enlightenment, it is helpful to keep in mind the line from the book of change: "The Dao that can be named is not the real Dao." With that disclaimer in place, the experience that I am longing for with my passing is essentially enlightenment. The process of letting go of the body at the time of the transition from this world to the next brings up the critical steps to experiencing enlightenment at a much higher velocity than we deal with in our daily practice.

Society almost has a mental illness in its common rejection of death and dying. It is inevitable that we all die in our bodies. Everything dies— the sun will die someday, trees die, animals die, and even rocks die. They will transform from rocks into sand, sand into dust, dust into raindrops, and raindrops into the ocean.

We all return to the ocean of our being.

Survival instincts don't just come when we are threatened. That fear is with us always, and it is the main obstacle to enlightenment. What is fear trying to protect in our survival instincts? It is our illusion of self, which we can call the ego. It's the false identity that I am only my body. Where there is fear, there can't be love. We must let our attachments to this false self die. Where there is fear, there can't be love, so letting go of ego and illusions of safety are very connected.

The spirit is eternal, and what is eternal is the truest. The experience of the truth of who and what we are is enlightenment, to me. The prerequisite to this experience is the transformation of our identity. There's an alchemical process here of transforming the impure into the pure, steel into gold. We are all somewhere on this spectrum. I believe when we are enlightened, this realization becomes self-evident.

In daily life, it is very challenging to get fears of the loss of the false self to surface to this extent. Terminal illness is the fast track to enlightenment if we choose to work with it in this way. Otherwise, it would take a very deep meditation practice or something similarly intentional. It is up to all of us to choose how we work with our life experiences, and where those fears will be called to the surface. In those moments, we have the opportunity to address those fears with compassionate awareness and convert them into love for the eternal spirit.

We are each given an independent, unique, indestructible spirit that exists in the nonphysical, and therefore is unaffected by the cessation of our physical form. Energy cannot be created or destroyed; it simply transforms from an embodied spirit to a spirit untethered to this world. Where do we go after that? We cannot know, but I have faith from my studies and soul-searching that we return to the source. I foresee it as the purest homecoming possible. There we regain a state of union that erases all self-doubt, all loneliness, and all earthly afflictions. When once again we are able to see the truth of our being. I understand it as a beautiful transformation.

I think about the famous Einstein quote, where he says "We must answer the question for ourselves, 'Is the universe a friendly place?'" Our answer to that question provides our most basic orientation to the world. We tend to see what we believe is there.

I remember the couple of times I had to go to the emergency room at the hospital in an ambulance and couldn't bring my communication device, because it connects to my wheelchair but not a hospital bed. I had to go into a totally new environment with new people who I can't communicate with beyond a blink for yes, and side to side with my eyes for no. If I believed the universe was an unfriendly place, it would have been a petrifying experience.

Love and liberation, two of my favorite words, are related or interlinked. As I can increase my ability to see the world and all its manifestations through the lens of love, echoing back to the world love through my expression, I am increasingly liberated.

With love comes the liberation from suffering.

As someone who has experienced abuse, I have had the tendency to take on the role of victim. That has been a really important role to let go of and replace with self-love, especially in relation to the disease process.

I am not a victim of my body.

I am not a victim of ALS.

I am not a victim of my circumstance.

I love that I can decide how I am going to frame my experience.

I love my existence, in that it provides me with the lessons I need to get to where I am going.

I decide that it all has a purpose, and by that free will, I can choose to love myself, my life, and my body's disease manifestation.

Through that, I find liberation.

Grace

Dissolve my fears of bodily death into the radiance of love.

Let there be only room in my heart for gratitude of the eternal

spirit.

Drifting with the ever-flowing river of changing forms and phenom-

ena,

may glowing clouds guide my descent into the abyss of the un-

known.

We knock but grace opens the door,

to realization and release from suffering.

Grace brings healing to the afflicted.

Grace brings truth to the seeker.

Grace brings the shore of salvation to the souls lost at sea.

By grace the transmutation of fear into love, as water into wine.

Grace and the unknown are kindred spirits in the cosmos,

both at home in the heart but alien to the brain

and its analyzed control.

Trusting the feet will land safely on the ground in the morning mist.

Faith in grace outshines doubt to anchor in the way of the heart.

To be received by God into the womb of the divine feminine

is the act of grace like nature's embrace of the deep forest.

Hail Mary, full of grace... Mother of God,

Pray for us sinners, now and at the hour of our death.

I don't believe in hell, so for me sin is not a condemnation, it's an invitation to become

a more complete human being through the soul's evolution. The last two lines are

from the Hail Mary. For me God is synonymous with the Dao, Creator, Great Spirit,

Unnamable womb of potential, Source of Love and Life, the unified quantum Field,

ecstatic Emptiness

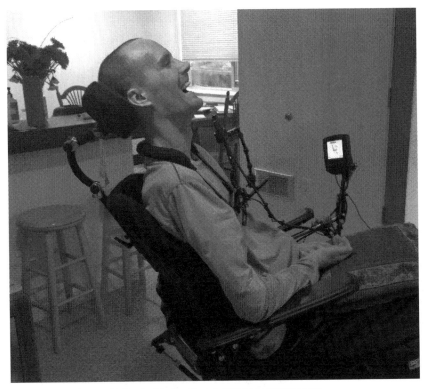

Dylan in his Portland, Oregon apartment

CHAPTER SIXTEEN

Let's Practice Dying

Vikki Voss
Dylan's mother

Dylan gives me books to read, and in one, the main message was to say over and over, "I don't understand," and that it's okay to be at peace with the mystery. So that's where I'm at with all of this—I don't have to figure everything out.

It's hard to think about dying, to really go there. But if Dylan is going through this, I want to go through it, too. Trying to imagine what that will be like has changed my life.

With this thought exercise, imagining it's your last days, the first thing that popped into my head after grieving my loved ones was regretting not doing more and having gratitude for Mother Earth. I want to do the right thing. And sometimes that means I stay longer at work and plod along until I get it right. Sometimes that means trying to make this event and that event for my students, but it's all stemming from this notion of how fragile life is.

I think I am following the Buddhist beliefs that this is a life of suffering, but at the same time, having an open heart, full of love and acceptance.

ॐ

I am not afraid of the cessation of my body containment, or death.

The language of dying doesn't align with my beliefs around that transition, so I tend to use words like passing—not away though, because conservation of energy, where energy can neither be created nor destroyed, is true for life as well as death. For me, passing is a returning home, to a nonlocal, atemporal realm of spirit that is superimposed with our physical reality, but only accessible to the highly evolved spiritual masters. Passing over when the body can no longer contain the spirit.

What a beautiful process, to have the veils of our warped perspectives of being overly attached to the physical reality cleared away, like returning from a dreary land with constant cloud cover—and behold, we are reacquainted with the warmth and brightness of the sun.

I am definitely not concerned with my prognosis suggesting that I will pass sooner than later. However, what my prognosis says about how I will cease my physiology brings up some red flags. Eventually, the muscles for breathing will become insufficient, and I will likely suffocate. Or I will get pneumonia and not be able to clear the fluid in my lungs and suffocate. One way or another, it is likely that I will have to transition from this body through suffocation.

I would like to say that I am more at peace with the projected progression outcome of ALS now, at least a little bit, but ultimately it seems that passing by suffocation is a serious challenge to maintaining a peaceful state of mind. It is a rather violent tearing of one from the breath of life.

But I still have time to train in equanimity.

It has always been my life goal to reach that state, but now it is a higher priority. Through my practice, I aspire to grow into my spirit such that even those strong cries of my body's survival instincts will be just leaves dropping on the ocean of my eternal Self. So full of love there will be no room to fear.

That aspect of fear is an ongoing project.

❧

Paul Kalnins
Professor and Clinician at NUNM

I think he's working on other levels right now, that won't be evident necessarily in this lifetime, but perhaps in the next and after that. This story might inspire others to say, "We are much more than just body, we are also spirit." In a way, the body is sacrificed to the spirit for higher development.

❧

In the fall of 2020, I had a wild night, to say the least. It happens rarely, but when it does it seems to catch me off guard. The eye camera didn't register my eyes when I woke up because the mucus in my lungs required suction. Further complicating the situation, the backup alarm had moved, making it unreachable. Again, this left me with no way to call for help. The mucus got worse over the next couple of hours.

Then, because my breath was obstructed, it set off the alarm on my ventilator. I had to keep my anger and blame in check, because I had talked to my mom multiple times about the need to take the alarms seriously. She has slept through most of them. One of the five times it went off, she got up to read the alarm notice and went back to sleep, forgetting the most important detail about the alarm: making sure I was ok.

So, I was on my own with my sensations of suffocation.

I prayed that I would be open to the lesson of the experience. I had to remind myself of the importance of staying calm, as my oxygen consumption goes up with my stress level, and limited air would only increase the sensations of suffocation. So, by the time my legs started to shake uncontrollably, I began to hold the intention that I would practice dying.

I prayed that I would be carried beyond my fears of death, being so unified with God that there was no room for fear. This intention was opposed by the judgmental thoughts that I had to turn away from fear gripping my mind. Only in that undesirable practice of facing my fears of mortality up close could I have this depth of soul training, without which I would surely not venture forward willingly.

Eventually, the camera started picking up my eyes again, and I was finally able to ask for suction, to breathe freely.

From this perspective, we have ample opportunities to connect with our higher nature, transforming what we have been taught to loathe by society into spiritual pushups, finding the deeper truths of our being through the body and whatever it manifests.

℃

Paul Kalnins
Professor and Clinician at NUNM

With Dylan's struggle, his body has failed, but he's growing in the spiritual sense. I think that is a very interesting insight that comes from anthroposophy, but several other traditions argue that our life forces are very active in early life. In the embryo, we grow our organs and a whole list of things, but that consciousness is constantly taking energy from our life processes. So, there's a polarity between consciousness and life. They're not the same. And in fact, to have more consciousness, we must take life from us. So… when you're busy, thinking all these things, you're sucking up life, you're sucking up glucose. You age the body, and then you have to sleep so consciousness leaves and the body can regenerate.

So, we're all undergoing that process.

What's happened for Dylan is a sped-up process where he's pulled life activities out, and he's working on other levels right now. His story might inspire others to recognize we are much more than just body; we are also spirit. He has learned lessons I think the average person will never learn in this lifetime or hundreds of lifetimes, because of [his] amount of suffering and the challenges. That creates a maturity on the soul-spiritual level that is accelerated.

In a way, the body is sacrificed to the spirit for higher development. And that, I think, will allow us to think differently in the future about these things. So that could be one message: The disease is a teacher. It's a process that evolves your consciousness. And I know a lot of people don't want to hear that. And you know unfortunately, a lot of people will say, "Well, you're shaming someone for having…xyz." No, it's not about that. It's about how there is this polarity between conscious and spiritual development and the body, and that it's something that we can't cure, but we maybe can balance.

We can start looking at how spiritual processes interact with the body. Different lives come into the world, learn lessons, grow, and then excarnate. We can talk about a life between birth and death, and a life between death and rebirth. And in our modern materialistic age, everyone is terrified of death. It's like that's the end—we have everything right now to get it in there before we die.

This is not the end of Dylan. If one message comes out of this, it's that the spirit doesn't die; this is not the end.

Instead of focusing on curing the body, how do we focus on Dylan's spirit? Let's not be so obsessed about the cancer that's going to kill us—let's be more interested in: did we clear up all that misunderstanding with our dad or our mom, or all those other karmic connections that we've made that we now have to carry with us into the next lifetime? We have the opportunity right now while we're still alive to work on those things.

Dylan, you don't have the body to go out into the world through your will, but now you can cultivate the will in an inner way. Through your thinking, through feeling. Keep trying as best as you can to share that with others while you can.

Willow Shanahan
Dylan's sister

I was honored that Dylan wanted me to be that person [to make the decision about his advanced directive]. Maybe he thinks I'm stronger than I actually am, though.

I talked with Trinity, one of his very close working doctors, and she calmed me down. Even though I'm that person the doctors are going to identify that he's in eye lock (when he can't move his eyes anymore), there'll be two doctors: one has to say that, yes, he is in eye-lock; the second one has to agree, and then we'll do the process from there.

I just didn't want to have to regret anything—to wonder, "Did I wait too long? Did I go too soon?" Scary things that you don't want to have to sleep with at night.

Vikki Voss
Dylan's mother

When I was giving birth to Dylan, I was singing this song; it's kind of hymnish: "Bless the Lord, Oh my soul..."

I don't even know if I know what the word "Lord" means anymore.

How about, "Bless the Love, oh my soul, and all that is within me, bless its holy name."

Dylan has made a funeral playlist, which is a little creepy to talk about, but I was thinking how cool would it be for Dylan to go out to the same song he came into this world with.

⁌⁌

Many people with ALS choose to end their lives because of declines in quality of life. Although the ventilator could keep us breathing for longer, other systems can become affected, and it can be too much to live with. Ten percent of patients will develop locked eyes, and without eye movements, we can't use the communication device that tracks our eyes.

I have already made it official that if I cannot communicate, it is time to pull my ventilator. It will only take a few minutes or less for me to suffocate. My doctor told me they usually give morphine to ease the sensations of suffocation.

Could I come to be so rooted in equanimity that I could go through this experience without the drugs? I'm under the impression that morphine will ease the grip of my survival instincts on me during the moment of truth, but it will also dull my embrace of my great return. What if, in the moment of reaching out to embrace the reunion with my maker, transcending the sensations that come with suffocating, I can experience a sense that something or someone is reaching back to me, welcoming me home? Even if it is only for a moment, to experience such a thing in waking consciousness would complete my spiritual quest in many ways.

Living in that state of dual awareness—of the physical and non-physical, spirit and matter—is the ultimate goal. But of course, I have no problem working towards that in my next life, having already cracked the seal in this one.

PART IV:

Being

I Say Peace

I say peace, I say peace to All

I say peace, I say peace to All

I say peace to my people, I say peace to my family

I say peace to my brothers and sisters throughout this galaxy.

I say peace to the ones bowing to Allah,

I say peace to the ones sitting with Buddha.

I say peace to the ones who pray to Jesus,

I say peace to the ones who kiss the ground beneath us.

I say peace to the blue collars, white collars, and small dollars,

I say peace to the big dollars of the corporate monopoly,

stopping me from playin that game,

It's all for love and not for fame.

I say peace to the Earth and peace to the Sun,

I say peace to the rebel and the soldier with the gun.

I say peace to the protests and peace to the war machine,

I say peace to the oil and the abundance of Green.

I say peace to the people with blood in their veins,

I say peace to the hearts of all to regain.

I say peace to our pasts, and peace to our future,

If not now, I'm sure to lose ya.

It's not a passive sit-back in the chair,

It's standing up and singing out for what's fair.

We can't let go and We can't give up.

We've got the faith and only love to share.

CHAPTER SEVENTEEN

What Would You Give Up?

Brandt Stickley
Professor at NUNM

I am moved by the tension and surrender that Dylan writes about so directly.
It's such a subtle disposition of mind, so nuanced and hard to grasp, but with
such a firm handhold on reality.

❧

Would I give up my experiences and lessons from living with ALS to walk again, to talk again, to sing and dance again?

Would I give up my experiences with ALS to be able to breathe on my own again, and not have to live with a tube in my throat?

Would I give up my experiences with ALS to eat food again, to taste and smell again?

Would I give up my experiences with ALS to fulfill my dream of being a doctor in my own clinic, teaching Aikido, having children?

Of course, I would.

Trail near Dylan's Portland, Oregon home

How could you not want to regain so much functioning, so many aspects of life, and only have to trade some intangible lessons?

Although, what part of me is answering that? The one that measures everything in terms of gains and losses is not my higher aspect. It is my ego or small self. Why would I stop giving up just ALS experiences—why not also the abuse from my father? And why would I stop there? At a certain point, I would have stripped away the experiences that have come to define me, that have shaped me into the person that I am.

If I answer the question from my higher self, I recognize that the hardships of my life and the challenges of living with ALS are indispensable to shaping me into who I am. From this perspective, these experiences and lessons are the cornerstones of my spiritual growth.

I don't believe that manifestations are random. As Einstein said, "God doesn't play dice." If one believes in a higher power—use whatever name—the truth is the same. All phenomena arise from the same source. I don't get to decide whether this manifestation is divine but not another. Faith is all or nothing. There is only one. It's our mind's judgment and dichotomies of good and bad that leads us astray by convincing us we know better. That was the forbidden fruit in the Garden of Eden after all.

The purpose of life is a lofty question, but I believe it is to grow into a more harmonious being of spirit and matter—to evolve as a soul to greater depths of love and truth, fully awakening our consciousness to the purest, most radiant reality. These hardships also provide huge opportunities for growth, as if equivalent to the challenge is the hidden potential for spiritual growth.

The lotus only grows in the mud, a diamond is only made under incredible pressure, and there is no rainbow without the rain.

These are hard truths and hard lessons, but I have faith that they bear fruit.

I'm on the highway to Buddhahood.

I can choose my destination in life, but to a large extent, not the pace. For me, that destination is spiritual awakening. I could have crossed paths with an enlightened teacher, but for now, I have the school of hard knocks—life challenges that intensify my experience to pressurize my transformation in the crock pot of my life.

More and more, if I can reside in my higher self, ALS is not my ene-my, it's my ally. So, the original question answers itself—no, I would not give this up.

That said, if there were a cure for ALS tomorrow that I could take going forward with all I have learned and experienced, I would. I'm not sadistic. But any wish beyond that would leave me fighting against my reality, fighting against myself, letting a desire to undo this ALS experience consume me. That voice has its place, and I keep it there. It is not all of me.

Humans are multi-layered, complex beings. Some of our most inspir-ing aspects come from our hidden and intangible elements, like our ex-periences and spiritual growth. Spirit is of the unseen, infused into all the physical world. The intangible experiences and lessons of our lives nurture the kernel of our soul to grow and blossom.

From that perspective, the original question could be, "Would I give up my soul to not have this disease?"

Of course not.

℘

Vikki Voss
Dylan's mother

You know, I think he would accept a miracle… I guess the miracle is accepting it all.

We are Heart

Take a retreat from the chatter of the mind and what's trending,

and quietly come into your heart space

to synchronize with the heart of humanity.

Spontaneously, without effort, nature's rhythm takes over,

like a silent snare drum of love, a mysterious pacemaker of peace.

Witnessing no number of cycles from leaf buds to fall colors

will satisfy my desire.

Freedom is in the moment's eternal presence

of our collective conscious heart.

The holographic heart holds the original image

in the cellular memory of the soul.

As winter yearns for spring,

the soul longs to return to its original image.

Stored in heaven,

reflecting into our being with all the bright warmth of the sun.

As above so below, above the sun of spirit,

below the ocean of being.

Resonating the cool waters of our being can calm global warming,

dissolve the hate of racism,

restore our forests, feed the poor.

The fate of the world depends on where we place our attention.

Take a retreat from the chatter of the mind and what's trending,

and quietly come into your heart space

to synchronize with the heart of humanity.

CHAPTER EIGHTEEN

Be More, Do Less

As a chronic overachiever and type A personality, I have historically associated my self-worth with what I could do, produce, or accomplish. When my right arm and dominant hand first weakened, I had to contend with the reality that I could no longer perform many of the tasks I was used to doing. After the diagnosis was official, I had to surrender to a future where I would be totally dependent on others for my survival.

Right up there with the fear of mortality was my perceived loss of the ability to be of service. I was so afraid to let go of my attachments to the role and career I had envisioned for myself. It was devastating to not be able to practice medicine as I planned after almost seven years of medical school. The fear of not being of service was worse than what was happening to my body.

Little by little, I learned to find new meaning in the process of decline. I began interpreting it as an invitation to be more and do less. This became my catchphrase.

Be more, do less.

At first glance, this may seem like a contradiction, as though by saying to "be more" I am saying we are not enough as we are. But it's precisely the opposite. Not "be more" as in increase what you are; be more as in be you more often.

Be more, do less.

Because in truth, being is a radical act of doing. And when you see the truth of it—the truth of being yourself—you can do anything.

ࡄ

Vikki Voss
Dylan's mother

Throwing myself in the fire—it's part of my personality that Dylan's always talking to me about. "You need to slow down." My job is not my worth.

This notion of being a scatterbrain? I think I'm really making headway in that. The chatter of the mind and what's trending... I'm trying to not be so frantic.

One time, I went and took a nap on his bed, and it was just what I needed. Just to share that space.

Tammy Staudt
Qigong Professor at NUNM

He's already there, right? There has just been a part that doesn't know he's there. That's where all this flow is coming through. He's already there. But there's still this part that's denying it out of habit on some level, which is the same for all of us. When you are there in the same way as when the writing is pouring through him, it just is. You're just in that space, and nothing else really matters. At that moment, you're in liberation. There are no other requirements.

ࡄ

Being of service had always been my purpose. That's why I had been working so hard for years to become a doctor, so I could really make an impact in the world. I chose naturopathic and Chinese medicine because those paradigms have the most to offer in terms of wellness, and liberating our full, vibrant potential. But when I was diagnosed with ALS, I had to

Dylan in the food truck he built, The Healthy Horse

reevaluate my purpose. Or at least reinterpret what it meant. What is the meaning of my life if I can no longer be of service? Why do I matter? Why am I here?

How can we begin to quantify the value of a life? First, we might rule out the obvious reasons why I don't benefit society.

I can't work, so the state pays for my food, ongoing medical expenses, and housing at a home that is staffed with nurses for people on ventilators. Medicaid has provided me with incredibly expensive equipment that facilitates my mobility and communication. The Department of Education has canceled the enormous student loans I took out to get through medical school. Clearly, I am not here to be a surplus contributor to the economic growth of our GDP (though I would argue purpose is never a mere cog in the wheel of the capitalistic machine). Neither can I justify my existence on some grand scale of productivity.

Everything I do is slow. I'm on a horse-drawn wagon in the face of the steam train in the Industrial Revolution. My mind might move at the speed of light, but my output is limited by my eyes and tablet interface. What was already a slow process of typing with my eyes has become even slower and laborious as I have developed problems with my eyes. Now I am not even on a horse…more like a mule. And a stubborn mule at that.

I aspired to become an author, although the current reality of such slow typing makes writing anything more of that length hard to imagine. It would need to be something short, hopefully dense with meaning and guidance—say poetry or a formula (a la $E=MC^2$). Still, there are many days that I am feverishly sick and cannot muster the energy to do much of anything. For now, it is reasonable to conclude that I will not benefit society by the many books I will leave behind.

With these physical struggles, what can I hope to tangibly give future generations?

In truth, equating our worth based on what we can produce is purely fictional—a falsified materialization of the soul and spirit. No one's value is dependent on what they can do, rather it's inherent in who they are.

Our worth is simply in being.

Being is doing.

It's futile for anyone to base their worth on what they can produce, make, or do. And yet that is precisely what we're taught. The reward model is so tempting, who can resist? Certainly, what we do is important and has value, but if we over-emphasize "doing" relative to "being," then those of us with disabilities or chronic diseases can never do enough.

But who can?

Be more, do less.

⁓

Patrick Shanahan
Dylan's uncle

My Prayer was: Please, God, give Dylan a spiritual experience that none of us will ever understand, I made that clear to him, and he understood what I was saying and always affirmed that it was what he was trying to do.

Shannon Curtis
Housemate and fellow graduate student at NUNM
I think my wish for him is the place that he's been at, that he's reached, and that I would love to reach someday.

Zac Marten
Roommate and fellow undergraduate student at Evergreen
That's so unique about somebody with ALS, you know—that they're physically so stationary. And I know Dylan, as stationary as he is physically, I know he has traveled so far in his spiritual realms. Like, way beyond. It's only going to increase.

ℰ℈

There is a section in the Yellow Emperor's Classic of Medicine, a foundational classical text of Chinese medicine, where it discusses two sustaining energy sources that enable our lives. One is called pre-natal energy, considered your essence and not readily replenished. Some say "You only have what you are born with." The other energy source is called post-natal energy, which has three sources. The first two are rather intuitive: we get energy from the food we eat and the air we breathe. The third source comes from living in accordance with our heavenly mandate.

Because of free will, I don't translate this energy source as destiny. Rather, that is what heaven wants for us, we naturally want for ourselves. This is not something we want with our ego, like wanting to be famous; it is something we want to live in our hearts. This heart's desire is what I am calling purpose. I believe our divinity is within our humanity: Your purpose is your path, and your path is your purpose. In Daoism, this is the way. When we are in sync with our purpose, it brings post-natal energy or Qi. I feel it as a spontaneous momentum in my life. When I am living my purpose, the path I am on moves with me, like an airport walkway.

My purpose has not changed, even though my circumstances have: I am still here to be of service, a large part of which is contributing to the awakening of the full capacity of human consciousness. I could ask myself, then, how does my current situation serve my purpose?

The intense busy schedule of my double doctorate programs left little time for esoteric practices like meditation and prayer. Now that I am living the hermit's life, I have ample opportunity. Similarly, writing has always been an indispensable outlet for my creative expression. I have plenty of time for that now, alongside the blessing of technology and eye movement. I have also explored unconventional avenues to utilize my medical training, like online health consulting with an emphasis on holistic wellness: body, mind, and spirit.

When I couldn't move my body, I connected with the nonphysical aspect of self, my inner source. This allowed me to unload the things that hid in my basement, things that caused me to feel like I was operating at a deficit, as though I needed to make up for some darkness of character. More and more, I began to feel that I could be whole and content with who I am. This was when I started to really feel a shift, and at the same time my friends started an online fundraiser and things got posted on Facebook. Love and support came pouring in when I finally gave it to myself.

Even though what I have gone through is so far removed from our typical experience it can seem unimaginable, I often recognize that the lessons I learn through my ALS experience are applicable to everyone. I like to say, that one door closes, two doors open. The possibilities are endless—it's all about how we frame circumstances.

A few years ago, I was an able-bodied individual about to begin a career as a doctor. And then I wasn't. That loss of identity and social status was paramount. Those are transient parts of our external validation and ego, which my circumstances dismantled in the extreme. But surpassing the death of my identity and status opened a new space in me, the space for more authentic identification as a human spirit. This level of surrender through my life and disease process benefits us all.

I may not be able to do everything I did before, certainly not in the same way. Nor can I do as much. But I can always find ways to serve. I have come to realize that in my state of being, I can be just as influential, if not more so than I could have writing prescriptions as a doctor.

❧

Donald Spears
Housemate and fellow graduate student at NUNM

In his way, he just says, "Keep doing the spirit of the medicine. You're doing it the right way, just keep going." I think that's one way that he has left the gift with me. It's like a part of him still exists in my treatment approach. And it will continue. Sometimes it feels like he's there helping me through some treatments. A part of who I am when I'm treating patients is a part of Dylan.

❧

I've always believed that my purpose in life was critical, but from when my symptoms started till now, it has literally become my lifeline—a North Star to guide me through the challenging terrain of life. No matter how dark the night becomes while drifting at sea, I am never lost. My North Star shines bright, guiding me as I steer my rudder. Living our purpose, living our Dao, is wind in our sails, the compass and momentum to reach that other shore.

With great hardship comes an equivalent potential for spiritual growth. Our ability to make use of the hardships through our purpose can be the path to survive anything, even thrive. We who live with incurable challenging diseases have tapped into resiliency and breathed it into the world. I can say that I have endured lifetimes of hardships, and now, because my life has been whittled down to the most essential elements, I have increased potential for growth and spiritual revelations.

My purpose allows me to reframe the most gut-wrenching experiences I've been through—like the general inability to move my body to practice the martial art I love, like the discomfort of living with a tube in my lungs, like the body terror of suffocating from accidents around my ventilator.

During that wild night when I was nearly suffocating for hours with no way to call for help, my clarity of purpose gave me the strength I needed. Even in the agony of that moment, I could see how being up close and personal with my fears of death was helping me grow. Accepting the reality of the moment with an open heart—resting in equanimity—showed me a reality beyond fear, a truth of myself—and all of us—beyond the physical realm.

Just as the birthing process is one of the most extraneous and painful experiences but also brings forth life, through my enduring such humbling and painful experiences, I too am birthing life into the world.

Like weeds growing up through cracks in the concrete, the life of consciousness emerges in our materialistic consumer culture.

And by sharing my experiences—both dark and light—I can continue to serve my purpose of serving others.

I am an exaggeration of universal truths, and that is what I offer the world. Extreme circumstances expand our awareness of what is possible. The contradictions of my life's experiences awaken our hearts to the power of our own potential, simply by being who we are and living in alignment with our unique purpose. We don't have to fight what is happening—we can use equanimity to be at peace, which brings us the energy we need for any circumstance.

On a more practical level, I am or hope to be, an example of contentment with living. Being alive is the supreme miracle. To be able to experience life in the full spectrum of its natural ebb and flow is the greatest gift. I try to keep that in mind every day. It helps me feel grateful for my existence—simply to be alive.

How would the world change if people were more content with their lives? What if we could appreciate the simple things? A sunset, the beauty of the changing seasons, a warm cup of tea with a friend, a meal with family, or a gentle breeze?

We take so much for granted. I matter to the world because, if I can be content with my life—if I can be at peace with what is—I can help change the tide. I can counter the black hole in the heart of our discontent society, that sucks the light from life. Call it the collective consciousness or reaching out with my feelings, but my continued appreciation for life while living in the most extreme circumstances aids our return to the universally shared purpose of spiritual growth.

The miracle of life cannot be bought or sold; it is only to be honored for the sacred gift it is.

The miracle of your life cannot be bought or sold; you have permission to honor yourself for the sacred gift that you are.

We are all people of implicit value—I hope my life clarifies this as a human being and not as a human doing. Even though I barely leave my home, the resonating truth of who I am as a Living Spirit is felt throughout the collective human consciousness.

One of my favorite quotes from Paul Selig reflects this: "The vibration you hold is how you serve." Slow as it is, I will continue to share what I have until I can't, and then I will simply be. My value approaches infinity as I approach the promised land, the spiritual spring of inner knowing that I am here. The purification and presence that I bring to the spirit of my circumstances ripple throughout eternity.

We're all open pianos—a sack of vibrating particles held together with quantum strings. I will always exist as a vibration in the world, emanating outward to others across space and time.

So will you.

I invite you to come resonate with my chord of peace and love.

Simply let yourself be.

∽

Mikael Brucker
Fellow graduate student at NUNM

One of our Qigong retreats—or maybe two, I can't remember—was at his childhood home. And I'm a naturopathic doctor, right? But I didn't grow up in nature. He did. He has a lifelong relationship with the woods around his house. And he was way more excited about showing us the woods than he was about showing us his house. He would share his refuges as well, because of all the difficulties with his dad. ...he would find solace in being out in nature.

That helped me to better understand how he is, and who he is... He was so excited to take us out into the woods.

Donald Spears
Housemate and fellow graduate student at NUNM

There are no trails there.

We must have been walking for a few miles, at least—off-trail, just through the woods...but he knew where he was going. I would have lost my bearings. I feel like I have a pretty good sense of direction, but not in that thick of a forest. Knowing that was his backyard...

I grew up in Southern California, where we have giant walls and small backyards. That was my backyard. His backyard was hundreds of acres. And he explored it all.

Shannon Curtis
Housemate and fellow graduate student at NUNM

When we forget our connection to nature, we forget our connection to other people, and we forget our connection even to ourselves. So that's a key part of returning to the medicine, is that reconnection. Having a community, having a place to have these beautiful, loving, supportive relationships is just the foundation for health.

I feel like the way we practice our medicine is constantly evolving, but it always comes back to the truth of who we are. And when I think back to how Dylan practices, that the truth is the medicine... He's always known it.

❧

Coconspirator

That's why I had to come here,

to hear my prayers,

to see the love,

with eyes as wide

as fresh carrot juice.

Dylan with mom Vikki, getting antibiotic therapy

The Way

一陰一陽之謂道.

The wholeness of Yin & Yang is called the Way.

繼之者善也, 成之者性也.

[What] follows from it is favorable, [and what] it shapes is of its

innate [imprint in clay].

仁者見之謂之仁, 知者見之謂之知.

The kernel of the human Heart sees it and calls it it's own,

while wisdom is seeing it and calling it known.

百姓日用而不知, 故君子之道鮮矣.

Common people daily use it but [are] unaware,

causing the completion of the nobleman's Way to be rare.

My professor didn't appreciate the liberties I took in my translation of this ancient

classical Chinese to make it rhyme. I stand by its artistic accuracy.

CHAPTER NINETEEN

Letter to a Friend

I wish I could remove the pressure you put on yourself to make yourself worthy of being. Feeling the love that is your birthright, unconditional love, and acceptance of the Creator is liberation. We are created in God's image, and therefore, our worth and value are implicit in our being, as living spirits.

Fostring freedom from moment to moment is the path of liberation.

Continuing to play those mind games, with an accruing interest in your divinity. Time is your vehicle of liberation. Staying present in the presence of the divinity that is all around us, fractal holograph, where everything is consubstantial, where everyone is consanguinity, makes the ancestral tree transparent by reciprocal perception.

When you perceive the divine, your divinity is perceived. Simply look and be seen.

And whether you are in your doing or sitting still, there is an open invitation to be in the presence of yourself and divinity. It is always the same game, to be in the felt presence.

Can you feel it? Is there anything more important? Not to the seeker. Although it is a misnomer to be seeking—like a fish seeks the ocean when it's always in it.

Imagine that originally there was no space or time, and then through God, all of manifestation came into being. Like God blew up a balloon to fill the universe. We are literally in God and of God. God's breath animates all things.

The keyword is in.

Are you in your body? Are you in your feelings? You are the wave-particle duality. All matter is the infinite potential of the quantum wave function. And the body knows its connection to source.

Through the body is the way of liberation from the pathological thinking that you are somehow less than, not in, not inherently worthy of love, separate, and not of the divine. No matter what you have done, nor any future action can change the fact that you are.

You are a full cup. You are the beauty of the world, bright shining as the sun.

Can you feel it? It is in there. It is in you, not out in the world. The way is to feel it in you. Every cell is coherent with the universe and every electron of the body.

You are a tuning fork with the whole spectrum of the seventy-two octaves of electromagnetic frequency available to you. You can choose your vibe.

Your natural state is harmonic resonance, birthing reciprocity.

Can you feel it?

The task is to play with staying present, feeling the presence of the divine, your divinity, and continually practicing.

Can you feel it?

From Dylan to Zac Merten, and also as a reminder to himself, and now as a reminder to the reader

Who is My Hero

I am. "I" as in my true self.

The person that I strive to be.

I am here deep inside myself covered with fears,

anxieties, and bad habits.

Underneath I am Pure.

I am the one who knows what actions and thoughts are good or bad

without having to even question it.

There is no questioning or answering, just being.

I know only happiness and to help others find happiness.

My life is a service to others.

That is my hero.

A true hero by every definition.

In this way, I don't have to replicate anyone

but circulate my own Ideals.

This perfection is what I aim for.

Sometimes I miss, but sometimes I hit right in the bullseye.

When I'm astray I can learn how, why, or who I am not.

This learning is a slow process,

especially when I forget the lessons I have already learned,

holding myself back from progressing to the next grade.

Each time I repeat the lesson,

I learn an even more in-depth version of who I am not.

Who am I?

 I am my hero.

written at age 20

CHAPTER TWENTY

Best Days

Tammy Staudt
Qigong Professor at NUNM

His story and this journey, on the outer, can appear like this huge punishment and taking away. And yet within that journey, you have this connection to light. This deeper expression and opening to possibility for all of us. To everybody's journey into a deeper acceptance, a deeper love, knowing our own value.

This, to me, is part of humanity waking up. I think we're in that right now, by all this chaos and all the shadows coming up. We're waking up. We're waking up to what has been there, we're waking up to new possibilities and new ways of relating and new ways of living, and this connection, this interconnectedness between us all.

Dylan's story offers a path. It offers a possibility.

❧

My best days are like watching these trees changing with the seasons. I can experience through them the shimmering leaves reflecting the morning glow in a gentle breeze. Even days of storming winds are a yoga stretching session for the branches and leaves.

My own chaotic expression is mirrored in the organic order of a higher realm, a string theory playing the chords of chaos on the keyboard of leaves. I almost understand the music, until I think I do.

It is consistently focused, living its truth, throughout all the seasons and varied weather patterns, growing towards the light.

To have a simple mission—to nourish life, spreading life with the massive gusts of pollen that the tree on the right put out a month ago when at that time the purple-leaved tree was all pinkish purple flowers.

When there are no leaves and all flowers, it reminds me of being a naked open book to the world, sharing my inner beauty without shame or self-judgment.

I'm a shelter for life, and families of little birds take refuge in my branches.

Since I don't move, I have a lot in common with these trees. The trees are motionless until this invisible force moves through them, animating them. I'm similar and will be stationary until this invisible inspiration moves in me with an idea to write a poem, article, or email to a friend. Then I can look back at what has danced across my screen and see the motion encapsulated in the word.

We dance in the wind together on those days.

In between the wind's dance, the changing weather, and the various climates of the season, I am content with my purpose, growing towards the light.

Free from notions of completion or pace. Knowing that there are sunny days that I can grow more, and days dark in the cold, I lean into stretches of stormy gusts.

My energy is maintaining the principle of "bend but do not break."

I am perfect in the variance, making use of what the universe presents.

Ring upon ring, circle upon circle, life upon life.

Perfectly, as it should be.

Growing towards the light.

Dylan with friend Zac Merton's son, Nolan

Evergreen Man

A song by Liam Shanahan, dedicated to his cousin Dylan

You never walked the beaten path,

but the light was always shining on you

And every choice you had to make was from a loving point of view

Like a bird across the sky, you used the wind to guide your way

Norml man can't keep a smile, but you did every single day

An evergreen man, a life on the move

Superman, you got nothing more to prove

You traveled the world and you left behind your love

You still gave a life's worth and then some,

even though you're bounded from above

There's not a tree you haven't climbed or a river bridge you haven't

built

Every flower has its time

But you're a rose that just won't wilt

And as a boy, you roamed around so fearless and free

The rising tide can lift all boats and you're the motion of the sea

Evergreen man, a life on the move

 Superman, you got nothing more to prove

you traveled the world, and you left behind your love

 And you still gave a life's worth and then some,

even know. You're bounded from above.

When the going gets too tough, and your body starts to fail

When you haven't got the strength, and your illness prevails

You can take a look around and notice what you see

But you're an angel to most and a hero to me

Evergreen man, a life on the move

Superman, you got nothing more to prove

You traveled the world and you left behind your love

You still gave a life's worth and then some,

 even though you were bounded from above

Yeah, you still gave a life's worth and then some,

even though you're bounded from above.

CHAPTER ZERO
Infinity

I grew up on an island in the southern tip of the Puget Sound, Harstine Island. It's mostly forested, with timber company wildland, and sparse residents around the main perimeter loop drive. This provided miles and miles of forest for me to explore on deer trails with my brother, and later with my sister when she got a little older.

Our favorite game was to pack a lunch and see how lost we could get. Since the road is a loop around the forest, we would try to guess which part of the island we would come out on.

As long as we walked straight, we knew we would always find the road home.

My Happy Place

Lying at the foot of the Giants.

Cushioned with a bed of moss below.

Covered above by the elders of ancient days

towering up towards the light.

There's a gentle breeze,

a soft rustling of leaves and branches all around.

The peaceful sound of a forest.

Content gazing up at the ceiling of branches swaying in the wind.

The deer off in the distance don't even catch my eye.

There are no demands, no external expectations,

no one to impress or let down.

No fear of failure, nor desire to be the best.

It's just the sounds of the forest with me in the center.

Grateful to be listening to God's symphony.

Still frame from Unfixed documentary

AFTERWORD

by Kimberly Kessler, Editor

We're all terminal.

Such a simple, irrefutable truth. And yet, while working on this project with Dylan, this turned out to be a major revelation for me. Now, for the first time probably ever in my life, the idea of death doesn't fill me with dread.

I've been affected by two extremes of death—the sudden, unexpected shock of my dad being killed in an airplane crash, and the gradual but unyielding decline of my stepdad to a brain tumor. Before this project, these losses served as my education about the realities of death. It was something to fear. Something to fight.

The thought of my own death or the death of a loved one often led to an existential spiral. I'd imagine everything, playing the movie out frame by frame: finding the body, breaking the news, planning the funeral, and then getting on with things sooner than you're ready to. When the spiral happens, it feels like I'm standing at a cliff, peering down at all of the potential nightmare scenarios I've ever imagined. To break free before succumbing to all-out despair, I have to imagine my higher self literally grabbing my neck and yanking me back from the edge.

Dylan's writing took me by the hand and led me to that same cliff, but this time the experience was serene. His words invited me to rest, to accept the limitations of our humanity, and to recognize death as nothing more than a phase shift, like ice returning water. Somewhere along the way, the ground beneath my feet became solid, and the nightmares were replaced by a sea, smooth as glass, stretching out before me to the horizon. It waits for me, not to sink into despair, but to choose to leave my mark. Death is just another ripple, not something to be feared.

I'd heard death spoken of this way before. Sort of. In church.

I grew up born-again, where everyone touted that "dying and going to heaven" was a Christian's greatest joy. All the church songs talked about dying as going home, in this saccharine, overzealous way, as though it would be such a relief to get out of here. It never made sense to me. Life is short and eternity is long—why be in such a hurry to leave? I actually got into an argument with my grandfather about it in my early twenties. I don't know if I ever recovered.

This preoccupation with what exactly happens after we die—and whether or not you have the cheat codes that lead you to the good ending—feels ridiculous to me now. Our desperate attempts to eradicate uncertainty only create more suffering. We create our own hell on earth.

That's what my view from the cliff used to feel like. It didn't feel like living—but immersing myself in Dylan's perspective, knowledge, and experiences did. Dylan's book brought me the comfort those songs were supposed to bring.

This project came to me at a pivotal time in my life. I was deconstructing my own identity, which had aligned so well with Dylan's early obsession with performance and achievement. His descriptions of trying to gain approval from others—and therefore find worth for himself—felt like second nature to me. The more desperate our attempts at control become, the more they lead to suffering, and then the cycle repeats again. It didn't matter how different our lives actually were, I felt like I was reading about myself.

With Dylan leading the way toward acceptance and subsequent peace, it wasn't just death I could embrace; it was life too. My life. Suddenly, I could believe something new.

Dylan so gracefully demonstrates how to hold space for ourselves amid our desperation, how to release our past—the trauma and the glory days alike—and detach from our futures. To relax our grip on the desire for a particular outcome or else. To simply and fully love ourselves, exactly as we are. Here. Now.

In truth, all we have is now.

No need to fear death or what comes after. No need to fear getting it wrong. There is only the present choice to create the kind of experience you want to have within the circumstances you've been given.

There is a surprising amount of power in this level of surrender, and it's a power each of us is born to wield. Not because someone else gives you permission, but simply because you exist. As Dylan reminds us, energy cannot be created or destroyed. You are a part of this universe, always have been always will be. Just...be. That's it.

Being is your birthright.

Unfortunately, we have also inherited a lot of misunderstandings. The gift that Dylan gave us by sharing his experience is the opportunity to re-learn, reimagine, and realize the meaning of words and actions. Of health, wellness, wealth, and loss. Of family and time. Of success and failure. Of being and doing. Love and not love. Life and death and life again.

The purest expression of free will is not merely our actions, but in the meaning we make of them. In how we choose to interpret the events of our lives and we can't get that interpretation wrong, at least not in the way so many of us were taught. No, this life is an experiment. We get to try on all its potential meanings. We get to seek and find our own unique paths out of the woods. We get to just be because we already "are" and are therefore enough.

This doesn't mean we have to waltz into death with glee. Death is change and change will always have its sting—just as life will—but pain isn't bad or wrong. It just is. The power to make meaning is the power of complexity—the power to let something mean everything and nothing at the same time. To feel the pain and grieve through it, without making anything about the process wrong or bad or weak or evil. It just is.

The awareness and acceptance of "what is" is the universal cheat code. It's what stops us from turning our pain into suffering by making it mean something it's not. This is what I wish I could have articulated to my grandfather back when we argued about the afterlife, although I couldn't put my finger on it at the time. Being present with truth and love is all any of us need to experience heaven. There is no escape from death, but there can be liberation from suffering. He surely understands this now, far better than I do, as he has already made his own transition to whatever comes next. I suppose the difference for me is that, for the first time in my life, I am not afraid of what that transition might be. Even if it's nothing at all, I know I won't be alone when it happens.

I AM terminal.

And so are you.

And it doesn't mean what we thought.

It only means what we want it to mean.

I don't know about you, but for me, that brings a sigh of relief.

We can't miss out on our own lives. We can't get any of it wrong.

So stop worrying.

Stop avoiding.

Stop arguing.

Stop performing.

And just be.

Or don't. Where you go from here is really up to you. I don't know what your path will look like. What I do know is that reading Dylan's words changed you in some way, big or small. It certainly changed me.

So I invite you to sit with that difference and embrace it. Love yourself as you were before you met Dylan, as you are now, and as you will become. Let yourself become. Let yourself just be, at least a little more often than you did before.

And when you inevitably get caught in the grip of doing—of hustling, achieving, performing, controlling—I invite you to stop.

To remember the power of stillness.

The power of your breath.

The power of seeking the Golden Middle of equanimity.

The power that exists within the mere vibration of your cells.

Reach out with your feelings, from your specific location in space and time.

Reach out with love and compassion for the matter around you.
Reach out,
and you will feel Dylan,
and all of those who came before,
and all those who are yet to come,
reaching back.
Together, we can experience the liberation of being.

Appendix

The following are a collection of additional poems—many written with the late-stage, diminished eye-muscle functioning of ALS when brevity and precision are paramount.

The Love Unknown

The lost love is tragic,

the missing piece of passion that could inspire magic.

But the love that is unknown,

the love that is my home will never be outgrown.

The pain we carry is the love we hold back.

I don't know what love is, or how to love from lack.

Just know it's a longing, a light surrounded by black.

An urge to reach out, plant's roots reaching for water.

Would you bother to leave the safety of the pack?

The pain we carry is the love we hold back.

All my fear, pain and lack.

Slung over my shoulder in the sack.

Oh, it's so familiar, similar, and obsolete,

a habit of self-deceit.

How pain becomes a comfort is a mysterious fact.

The pain we carry is the love we hold back.

We see the path of pain but still we travel it.

Never thinking that we could unravel it.

Habits

Habits are the forms that hold us.

I pray that your cells are solid with the light of truth.

For when the time comes for surrender, who upon do we lean?

Chaos

Calling out to chaos.

Is my voice recognized in its melody?

Entropy is to me like fires are to the forest,

designed ecology.

Though in the chorus we repeat a certain message,

specific to our intent among the infinite.

Rainfall's descent carries chords of the silent.

APPENDIX   218

A Place to Call My Home

Where, oh Lord, can I lay my bed?

Where, oh Lord, can I rest my head?

All I need is a place to call my home.

Where, oh Lord, can I lay my bed?

Where, oh Lord, can I rest my head?

All I need is a place to call my home.

It's a crime that a few say they own it all.

We're born into this world without a right to land.

We're forced to trade our life for their money.

Then give it back to them to fulfill their plan.

Keeping us lost, lonely, and without a clan.

Where, oh Lord, can I lay my bed?

Where, oh Lord, can I rest my head?

All I need is a place to call my home.

Where, oh Lord, can I lay my bed?

Where, oh Lord, can I rest my head?

All I need is a place to call my home.

This earth is my body, yours and theirs.

How could you say you own the sun?

I'm traveling, wandering, looking for open space,

through cities and forests of grace.

It's all been claimed by the end of a gun.

I fear not death, for then home is the only center of a circle.

It's only here that we've created this unequal, unjust sequel of alien invasion.

This greeds got a hold of our cooperation,

compassion for each other, striving to be someone, somewhere you're not.

Didn't you know that mortgage stands for the knot of death?

Where, oh Lord, can I lay my bed?

Where, oh Lord, can I rest my head?

All I need is a place to call my home.

Where, oh Lord, can I lay my bed?

Where, oh Lord, can I rest my head?

All I need is a place to call my home.

The rules were rigged before we had a voice.

To oppose the system's oppression of choice,

Whether or not to play along.

For I give up, I'm climbing out of this hole.

This human system is built on chains of control.

I'm living in the domain spirit,

God's love, Buddha's peace and Allah's arms unfolding freedom.

No borders, titles, rent, or lease.

We've got to back out of this struggle and stand for peace.

Its got to change, these chains won't fit around my child's feet.

We've got to start this ball rolling.

So at least they can fly from this seat

of no place to call their home.

 Where, oh Lord, can I lay my bed?

Where, oh Lord, can I rest my head?

All I need is a place to call my home.

Where, oh Lord, can I lay my bed?

Where, oh Lord, can I rest my head?

All I need is a place to call my home.

A Sage Breathes Through the Heels

Breathing through the heels the sage ascends.

As Christ levitates on the conversion of water to wine,

sap is the body's suction from root to branch,

in line light follows the breath,

free of gravity.

Can you feel it rise?

Be the Echo

Be the echo,

as these hills are spoken through.

Let it voice your name.

Move your fingers across my palm

And feel the pulse of the universe.

(I wrote this during a bicycle touring adventure from Washington to Alaska)

Curse of Being Right

Even when I am clouded by judgments,

Seeing only what serves my predetermined conclusions,

Blame is a self-fulfilling prophecy,

Eating from the forbidden fruit of right and wrong.

For I am a vessel of endless forgiveness.

Or if I banish myself from myself,

I might be isolating in loneliness,

But I am right.

Divine Love

The light in my eye is blinding

and nothing that I am finding

is as desiring

as the love in your eyes.

And here we sit, late,

Contemplat'ing, remembering

to sing a song for you.

What is true, in the dark blue sky?

Time goes by, by and I try,

to feel you kiss me in the morning sun.

Fear undone for only fun,

behind to run for more to come.

What is small simple and sound,

goes all around the two of you?

You want a clue?

Something profound, but surely true.

Not from me,

you'll have to see

with your own eyes.

I touch your thighs,

give you a shiver that shakes and makes

you call out my name.

The same game.

Looking at autumn leaves, leaving the trees.

I drop myself to sacrifice for your health.

For winter music reminds us of the silence,

the patience, tomorrow will bring.

And Mama will sing in spring.

With a drop of lavender, I'll be your king,

If you be my queen, the scene of the setting sun

reminds us that summer has already come.

Written when I was twenty years old. It's my favorite piece of writing from this period of my life. After working on it late in to the night I had branched off into three different ideas. The next day was a collaboration with the universe, full of synchronicities to bring it all together. An event heavily decorated with purple or lavender for a departing staff member of my college earlier in the day, and then watching the sunset on that autumn day.

Gebser's Time Freedom

And as the light glistens the branch,

It forebodes death from the shadow.

Pressed up against the edge,

The mind attempts to flee,

Knowing it can't follow.

There is no reasoning

prespace and pretime,

Before the big bang there is neither,

And either are infinite in the hereafter.

Before and after don't live in the present.

I'm sinkin' or rowin'

I was feeling lonely working hard up on the hill

So I decided to go down, see a friend and chill.

It was the Saturday before I was coming to see you

 a fine day of June by the number of two.

Before I came to you with a song I would sing

I was going to the mountain to do some snow boarding.

I only took a break for a little while

Yeah but time keeps flowin,

so I'm either sinkin or rowin

Stepped out of life slow and asked for a cup

Drank it down with a cloud of smoke and got all messed up.

Then out came to mic and they started rappin

No one was really flowing but their feet kept tappin.

The words they were spitting weren't heard in mass

Talking about how I'm gonna kick it up your _____.

I only took a break for a little while

Yeah but time keeps flowin,

so I'm either sinkin or rowin

That night I ate like I was going to hibernate

Sure enough next afternoon I woke up at 4:08.

Well I didn't go riding on the great Mt. Hood

And I didn't come see you like I said I would.

I'm embarrassed to say but I went back that day

To hide away, to pretend to play.

I only took a break for a little while

Yeah but time keeps flowin,

so I'm either sinkin or rowin

I told myself I'd see you tomorrow

sing you some songs to ease your sorrow.

Then tomorrow came with a cloud in my head

The whole day I wished I was in bed.

I figured I'd stay home and use the day to rest

Cause I only wanted you to see me at my best.

I only took a break for a little while

Yeah but time keeps flowin,

so I'm either sinkin or rowin

This morning I drink water till it came out my ears

Trying to help my voice sound a little more clear.

Lunch break came and I borrowed a car

The drive to see you was not that far.

Put the guitar in the passenger seat

Thinkin oh boy you're in for a treat.

I only took a break for a little while

Yeah but time keeps flowin,

so I'm either sinkin or rowin

I was warming my voice up the whole drive

Hoping my song makes you feel happy to be alive.

Arrived at the hospital and park the car

Grabbed the guitar and strolled in like a rockstar.

Stop by the spiritual care room and ask for a blessing

Said a quick prayer and I was ready to sing.

I only took a break for a little while

Yeah but time keeps flowin,

so I'm either sinkin or rowin

I took the elevator to the fifth floor

Walked over to his room and looked in through the door.

It was empty, fresh made bed and all.

With a lump in my throat to the nurse I did call.

I asked if you were on your way to heaven

She said, "No", he left this morning at seven.

I only took a break for a little while

Yeah but time keeps flowin,

so I'm either sinkin or rowin

Well I knew you said you might be leaving today

I just figured it would all turn out to be OK.

In a way it did, because I wrote this song

And if you're listening, you might not come along.

Cause if I could, I go back to that Saturday night

Oh, I'd turn the other way without a fright.

 I only took a break for a little while

Yeah but time keeps flowin,

so I'm either sinkin or rowin

I only took a break for a little while

Yeah but time keeps flowin,

so I'm either sinkin or rowin

written at age 20

Map Maker

Map Maker, Map Maker please take a rest
Your goal of gold isn't really the best
Boats built of glass, fueled by oil, coal, and gas
We'll pass, cause this boat 's bound for glory

Our goal is glory, to tell our own story
No need to fight, nor horde inventory
there's enough for you, and enough for me
with our faith in the human family

Map Maker, Map Maker we seek no blame
nor to punish them bringing any one shame,
but we can't refrain for realigning the aim.
It's our claim, that this boat 's bound for glory

These ways of the world, we've been lazy to learn
The map maker said "Take a right at the turn,
The ships with sails are too slow for the pace
Use my oil, fire desire, to win the race!"

Map Maker, Map Maker let go of the wheel

With the winds still blowing, we'll sail with the seal

The whales, and sharks, running under the keel

What a feel, cause this boat 's bound for glory

Sailing to the seas that are yet unknown

Setting the compass by the pure heart tone

Until the truth is felt deep down in the bone

We might be lost but we're never alone

Map Maker, Map Maker please take a rest

Your goal of gold isn't really the best

Boats built of glass, fueled by oil, coal, and gas

We'll pass, cause this boat 's bound for glory

Our goal is glory, to tell our own story

No need to fight, nor horde inventory

there's enough for you, and enough for me

with our faith in the human family

Water

Water, cold water,

With a life of its own.

Through all phases of form.

Gas, liquid, plasma, and solid.

Speaking a language of its being,

Our Being, of water.

Source.

Indifferent and at the same moment ultra-resonate.

All vibrations heard in the sounds of water.

Speak to me, and I will listen.

The choice is my existence

Atemporal World

Forgiveness lies in the eyes of the beholder..

Disappointment is a direct result of expectations.

In action and rest, the divine art of Purpose.

Habits are the forms that hold us. For when the time comes for

surrender, who upon do we lean?

Living a lie is dying each day.

Sure, all life is dying,

But the rate of decay

Is a choice of Way.

Remember that there is no adventure without the unknown.

My story has no end in the atemporal world

Spring

The hope of early Spring blossoms,

fresh green sprouts of endless possibility,

resurrecting the eternal youth of joy.

Coming back from the cold fear of the dead of winter.

The winds of changing pressure and temperature

blow out the decrepit ideas of the past,

the illusion of separateness spawning greed and hate,

the fallacy of linear time fostering temporal entrapment

and fear.

Bright vibrant greens signal that bright new days are on the horizon.

Grateful for each warming day and the return of the season of plenty.

Letting the stamina of freedom envelope you,

everywhere freewill.

Choose a day to embrace your liver and feel the love of life returning.

Any day, all days,

lovingly Spring.

Acknowledgments

Thank you to all my generous Go Fund Me donors:

Adam Dombrowski, Adriana Collins, Amanda Watters, Amy Homer, Andrea Lewis, Andrea Negron, Antonia Wibke Heidelmann, Aubrey Garner, Audrey Ulrich, Aurelia Leroux, Barbara Diane Owens, Benjamin Gitchel, Brad Lyman, Brian Shanahan, Brooke Love, Burke Long, Cassandra Arora, Chie Aizawa, Christopher Edler, Claire Erhart, Claudia Eilers, Colin Gabriela, Siegfried, Colleen Brand, Connie Jones-Voss, Connolly Ann, Craig Mehrmann, Cynthia Curtis, Cynthia Schneider, Dana Chynoweth, David Kimble, Diane Saunders, Elizabeth Bogren, Ellen and Octavio Sanchez, Ellerie Nagy, Elli Harron, Emily Garclich, Eric Sund, Ernesto Salinas, Gigi Olsen, Gloria Rangelova, Gloria West, GoFundMe Team, Greg Becker, Heather Buser, Heather O'Malley, Heidi Hillman, Helena Escalante, Hye Yeon KIM, Ian Wilson, Jan Van Weesep, Janeen McLaughlin, Janet Ohanesian, Jared Casey, Jeanne Arnold, Jeffrey Erb, Jen Salazar, Jennifer L Abele, Joel Voss, John Anderson, John Novack, Joseph Delikat, Joshua Park, Julie Anding, Justin Marchant, Justin Oswald, Karl Black, Karl Stickley III, Karla Stockton, Kaylie Lutsky, Kelly Hoover, Kelsie

Hammitt, Kevin Costello, Kevin Mccormick, Kevyn Carothers, Kim Van Bruggen, Kimberly Warner, Kirsten Warner, Kitty Alaily, Krista Walker, Lars Fjelldal, Laura Watson-Sears, Lauren Mangat, Laurie Mabbott, Laurie Porter, Liam Shanahan, Linda Beck, Linda D'Alonzo, Lindsey Barbee, Lita Buttolph, Maitri Edwards, Margaret Wright, Margo Eytinge, Marian Husted, Martel Catalano, Melody Auseth, Michael and Bern Mackin, Michael Rosales, Mike Bachich, Nancy Gray, Nancy Warner, Nicola Corl, Noelle Stello, Patrick Shanahan, Patti Tupper, Paulina Larson, Pete Voss, Polly Moyer, Rebekah Phillips, Rene Morales, Rich Brauer, Rochelle Lisner, Ryan P Hofer, Sandy Brunner, Sandy Musclow, Sara Davidson, Sarah Veasey, Sayaka Yokota, Serena whitridge, Seth Truby, Shala Look, Shaler Wright, Shannon & Dave Wixted, Shannon Curtis, Shannon Kennedy, Shawna Zierdt, Sumiko Yagihashi, Tai Shanahan, Tanya Hill, Ted Bagley, Thomas Beben, Trevor Knight, Usman Ally, Vicki Look, Vickie Gonzales, Vikki Voss, Vida Long, Yvonne Meziere, 亮 中戸

Thank you to all the kind hearts who were willing to be interviewed for the book:

Adam Drombroski, Brandt Stickly, Donald Spears, Liam Shanahan, Mikael Brucker, Patrick Shanahan, Paul Kalnins, Rachael Karlin, Roger Batchelor, Shannon Curtis, Tamara Staudt, Willow Shanahan, Vikki Voss, Zac Merten

And a special thanks to my publishing team:

Brennan Sirratt, Dee and Dan Kerr, David McLaughlin, Kimberly Kessler, Kimberly Warner, Rodney Outlaw, Zac Merton

Made in the USA
Columbia, SC
13 August 2024

39938309R00141